To ...
with thanks of
your ministry
Ted Schroder
June, 2012

REAL HOPE

Also by Ted Schroder

Inward Light

Buried Treasure

Surviving Hurricanes

Solid Love

REAL HOPE

TED SCHRODER

Amelia Island Publishing
Amelia Island, Florida

2011

Library of Congress Control Number
2011909433

ISBN-13: 978-0-974-80866-6

Cover art: JoAnn Speas
Cover design: Axia
Technical assistance: Betzy Mitchell

Amelia Island Publishing, Inc.
15 Hickory Lane
Amelia Island, Florida

Printed in the United States of America

For my children and grandchildren

I will pour out my Spirit on your offspring,
and my blessing on your descendants.
Isaiah 44:3

The promise is for you and your children, and for all who
are far off – for all whom the Lord our God will call.
Acts 2:39

INWARD LIGHT
"....bracing and refreshing." **James I. Packer**

"...the product of profound understanding of the human heart, and prolonged reflection....keen observation and vivid style." **John Stott**

BURIED TREASURE
"...a splendid analysis both of faith and of the Apostles' Creed, unpacking its riches phrase by phrase and illuminating his text with a wide variety of stories and anecdotes....should be a great help both to seekers and new Christians. I have much enjoyed reading it myself and heartily recommend it to others." **John Stott**

SURVIVING HURRICANES
"..tells the truth about life – life's pervasive precariousness. It comes equipped with a phalanx of supporting literature, stirring but not sappy real-life stories, and a dark undercurrent of canny perceptiveness." **Paul Zahl**

SOLID LOVE
"...invites us to ascend the summit of Paul's eternal poem of love. You'll find practical and inspirational instruction in these pages." **Max Lucado**

"This is a most helpful and thorough study of love, biblically and practically. This book may make you squirm at some places. But it will lift your heart with hope that we may love as God in Christ has loved us." **Leighton Ford**

CONTENTS

INTRODUCTION

"**If** you were wrecked at sea on an island and a single chapter of the Bible washed up from wreckage, which would you like it to be?" Dr. Ralph Keiper reported five of twenty said Romans 8. Charles Hodge called Romans 8 "a rhapsody on assurance."

"If Holy Scripture was a ring, and the Epistle to the Romans a precious stone, chapter 8 would be the sparkling point of the jewel." Philipp Jakob Spener (1635-1705)

"Romans 8 is without doubt one of the best known, best-loved chapters of the Bible," wrote John Stott. Douglas J. Moo has called it the "inner sanctuary within the cathedral of Christian faith."

Tony Campolo writes: "This particular chapter is one of my favorites and over the years its verses have provided me with more texts for sermons than any other section of Scripture. It is a chapter that, for me, addresses almost all the components of a holistic theology."[1]

---

[1] Tony Campolo, *Stories That Feed Your Soul*, Ventura: Regal 2010, p.18

What is it that is so special about these 39 verses? The theme of the chapter is hope. Paul continually mentions the importance of faith, hope and love. Hebrews 11 is the "faith" chapter of the New Testament. 1 Corinthians 13 is the "love' chapter of the New Testament. I maintain that Romans 8 is the "hope" chapter of the New Testament. It is the prescription for the hopelessness that characterizes these troubled times. I write at a time of earthquakes, tsunamis and revolutions in the Arab world. It is a time of economic turmoil with government budget deficits, high unemployment and declining real estate values. Many people have lost hope in finding work and in selling their homes.

What is hope? Hope must be rooted in reality.

What is hope? It is not wishful thinking that hopes against hope for that which flies in the face of reality. It is not just optimism, which will not face up to sober evidence. It is not the same as expectation, which implies a high degree of certainty based upon what obviously is going to happen. "For in this hope we are saved. But hope which is seen is no hope at all." (Romans 8:24) We must have some basis, some reason, to hope. Hope must be rooted in reality. I believe in the reality of divine redemption: the saving purpose of God in Christ and the work of the indwelling Spirit. That is why I call what Paul describes as "real" hope. It is the anticipation of victory over sin, guilt and death. It is the belief that, in Christ, we can be conquerors in the battle of life. That is why Paul concludes the chapter in v.37 with the cry of triumph:

"we are more than conquerors through him who loved us." It is the answer to depression and despair.

Why do we experience so much depression in our society? Dr. Armand Nicholi, associate clinical professor of psychiatry at the Harvard Medical School and Massachusetts General Hospital maintains that many young people today feel that their cultures fail to provide answers to questions of purpose and meaning and destiny. "We fail, they feel, to provide some reason for hope."[2]

The causes of depression and hopelessness.

Two people who have influenced our secular society more than many others are Karl Marx and Sigmund Freud. Both attacked belief in God. Both men died bitter and disillusioned with little compassion for humanity. Both had virtually no friends. "As one reads about the ends of their lives – of how they finished the course – one notes an overwhelming sense of despair and hopelessness....Though they experienced extensive hardship and adversity, they apparently lacked the spiritual resources to enable them to finish the course with any sense of hope." Modern secularists are their heirs. Their influence can be seen in the deletion of any mention of Christian faith in modern movies and novels.

Dr Nicholi analyzes what he considers to be the causes of depression and hopelessness. "What often appears to be the cause of despondency in many today is an awareness of the gap between what they think they *ought* to

---

[2] Armand Nicholi Jr., Hope in a Secular Age, in *Finding God at Harvard*, ed. Kelly Monroe Kullberg, IVP, 112-120

be and what they feel they are. That is, there is a discrepancy between an ideal they hold for themselves, and at times think they measure up to, and an acute awareness of how far short they fall from the ideal."

"Other causes of depression are associated with loss: loss of a friendship, a job, a loved one, or a broken engagement or marriage, etc. Loss usually results in grief or mourning, a normal type of depressive reaction, relatively short-lived, self-limited, and not usually requiring medical help. Many, however, suffer depression without an associated loss. And in these people the cause often appears to be the disparity between what they ought to be and what they fear they are."

"An additional characteristic of depression is the feeling of hopelessness: the feeling that there is no way out, that things will only get worse, and that one is completely helpless."[3]

Guilt Feelings

Dr Nicholi asks, "What causes these universal feelings of worthlessness?.... In our society, moral and ethical guidelines have become less and less clear, and people's consciences less and less discerning. People nevertheless feel guilty about their behavior…I have observed many college students who express surprise that their actions produce feelings of guilt. They say that they have thought clearly about what they are doing and can give good reasons why they think specific behaviors are not wrong. Yet for reasons they don't understand, they feel

[3] Ibid.

guilty and worthless when they break the traditional moral code. We have already begun to accumulate clinical data that clearly demonstrate that this moral code which has survived the centuries provides guidelines that enhance individual dignity and ensure the greatest pleasure and the greatest good to the greatest number of people. One thing we know: when a person transgresses these guidelines, he or she will, sooner or later, experience feelings of guilt and worthlessness."[4]

All these symptoms of our spiritual condition are addressed by St. Paul in Romans 8. The gap between what we ought to be and what we feel we are is the theme of Romans 7.

The prescription to remedy depression and hopelessness.

"I do not understand what I do. For what I want to do I do not do, but what I hate I do. And if I do what I do not want to do, I agree that the [moral] law is good. As it is, it is no longer I myself [my new Christian nature] who do it, but it is sin living in me [my sinful nature]. I know that nothing good lives in me, that is, in my sinful nature. For I have the desire to do what is good, but I cannot carry it out. For what I do is not the good I want to do; no, the evil I do not want to do – this I keep on doing. Now if I do what I do not want to do, it is no longer I who do it, but it is sin living in me that does it. So I find this law [principle] at work: When I want to do good, evil is right there with me. For in my inner being I delight in God's [moral] law; but I see another law

---

[4] Ibid.

[principle] at work in the parts of me, waging war against the law of my mind." (Romans 7:15-23)

What is the prescription to remedy this spiritual condition of depression and hopelessness?

"I've tried everything and nothing helps. I'm at the end of my rope. Is there no one who can do anything for me? Isn't that the real question?

"The answer, thank God, is that Jesus Christ can and does. He acted to set things right in this life of contradictions where I want to serve God with all my heart and mind, but am pulled by the influence of sin to do something totally different." (Romans 7:24,25 *The Message*)

This is the spiritual diagnosis of the human condition in the New Testament. It describes the conflict in each one of us between the 'flesh' and the spirit; the two natures or principles within us.

Reassurance of our future and our hope.

In Romans 8 Paul gives us his remedy to the human condition. His diagnosis in the preceding chapters leads to his treatment of our condition of spiritual schizophrenia, the war between good and evil in us, the weakness of our moral center, and the continuing infection of self-centeredness that causes our hopelessness and despair.

"With the arrival of Jesus, the Messiah, that fateful dilemma is resolved. Those who enter into Christ's being-here-for-us no longer have to live under a continuous, low-lying black cloud. A new power is in operation." (Romans 8:1,2 *The Message*)

Over 39 verses Paul expounds how this power furthers the purpose of God in us and in all creation. It is a staggering vision of a universe remade and our part in it. It is meant to reassure us of our future and our hope. It takes us from our individual struggles to our cosmic destinies. It shines light on what God is doing in a suffering world. It encourages us to persevere in the face of difficulties and discouragement. If God is for us, who can be against us? Then we can know the unexpected and incredible truth that in all things God works for the good of those who love him.

Read through Romans 8. It is rich fare – not for the faint-hearted, nor for those of a delicate digestion. It is strong meat, not baby food. But if you can ruminate upon its truth, and absorb its nourishment into your life, you will be richly rewarded with real hope. That was Paul's desire for his readers, as he expressed, in this blessing, at the end of his teaching.

"May the God of hope fill you with all joy and peace as you trust in him, so that you may overflow with hope by the power of the Holy Spirit." (Romans 15:13)

1

NO CONDEMNATION

"Therefore, there is now no condemnation for those who are in Christ Jesus, because through Christ Jesus, the law of the Spirit of life set me free from the law of sin and death. For what the law was powerless to do in that it was weakened by the sinful nature, God did by sending his own Son in the likeness of sinful man to be a sin offering. And so he condemned sin in sinful man, in order that the righteous requirements of the law might be fully met in us, who do not live according to the sinful nature but according to the Spirit." (Romans 8:1-4)

As noted in the Introduction, Dr Armand Nicholi describes psychologically, "What often appears to be the cause of despondency in many today is an awareness of the gap between what they think they *ought* to be and what they feel they are. That is, there is a discrepancy between an ideal they hold for themselves, and at times think they measure up to, and an acute awareness of how far short they fall from the ideal."

Feelings of failure and loss.

The Bible has a word for this condition: it is one of the words we translate for "sin". The Greek word '*hamartia*' means missing the mark, or falling short. It means aiming for something and missing it. It is like lining up your ball on the 18th green. If you sink your putt you will win the match. If you miss it, you lose. You aim, putt ...... and miss! You know the sinking (no pun intended) feeling of failure. It is the word St. Paul uses in Romans 8. It describes failing to keep the commandments, failing to keep the covenant with God, failing to live the life God created us to live, failing to live a full, flourishing human life. It is the awareness of the omissions in our life: the things which we have not done which we ought to have done. Its symptoms are feelings of loss: loss of joy and peace, which manifest themselves in free-floating anxiety, and despair. Failure robs us of self-worth. Failure takes away our sense of dignity and value. We feel that we have somehow messed up and are worthless. Failure makes us admit that we are imperfect, which is a hard pill to swallow. It is having to say we are sorry – which is the hardest word to say.

Anyone who is aware of God's pattern for our lives, of what we are meant to be, by reading the Scriptures, and looking at the life of the perfect Man, Jesus Christ, realizes how far short from that ideal is the reality of our daily life. Our conscience accuses us, our relationships bear witness to misunderstanding, lack of love, insensitivity, and just plain hurtfulness and disappointment. When we look at the world around us we see what people do to one another. Greed, selfishness, cruelty and violence stalk the earth. Jesus said that the source of the problem is to be found in the human heart. "What comes out of a man is what makes him 'unclean.' For from within, out of men's hearts, come evil thoughts, sexual immorality, theft, murder, adultery, greed, malice, deceit, lewdness, envy, slander, arrogance and folly. All these evils come from inside and make a man 'unclean.'" (Mark 7:20-23) 'Unclean' is the biblical word for being unfit to walk with a holy God.

Spiritual death: losing hope in future goodness and happiness.

This is the human condition. We are all sinners, falling short of God's pattern for our lives. As a result, we suffer from the consequences of sin, which the Bible calls 'death.' Not biological death, which is natural to physical life, but spiritual death, death as the wages of sin, which means separation from God's presence and all that it entails. In Genesis 3 it is described as being banished from the Garden of Eden, far from the tree of life. It is being condemned to live out our lives without the blessing of his presence and purpose. It is being alienated from his fellowship. It is to be vulnerable to all that threatens our wellbeing. It is to lose hope in future goodness and happiness. It is to experience a diminishment of life, rather than life in all its fullness. It is to live in the kingdom of darkness rather than the kingdom of light. Death reigns over all humanity, and the fear of death poisons all human relationships with the anticipation of bereavement and loss.

We attempt to break out of this state by trying hard to live out our lives on God's terms. We try to be good, to do good, to earn praise, to find value in our lives, but all too often our attempts to be good, and to do good, to live up to our expectations either causes pride, and self-deception about our true nature, or else a realization that we still fall short of what we should be.

"I used to have a recurring nightmare that I was falling down a cliff."

I found myself in such a state in my teenage years. I knew the commandments, I attended church. I learned about Jesus. I was aware of what a Christian life was supposed to be like. I tried very hard to live up to those ideals. I wanted to be the best person I could possibly be. I wanted to fulfill my potential. But I constantly failed, and disappointed myself. I was consumed by guilt. I rarely seemed to be able to satisfy my parents, my teachers, my coaches, or other significant people in my life. Was it just my low self-esteem, a pattern of family perfectionism, or was it a symptom of the human condition? Why is it that this theme pervades literature which deals with human experience?

I used to have a recurring nightmare that I was falling down a cliff. Not until I discovered that it was an unconscious fear of failure was I able to overcome it.

When dear members of my family died I felt the hand of death upon me. Death seemed to take away from me those who meant more to me than any others. What was the point of life if the people you loved disappeared without explanation, and without trace. Where did they go? What was life all about if we are here today and gone tomorrow?

Are we condemned to live out our days under a sentence of death, with nothing to look forward to except annihilation and oblivion? But how could that be when life was so full of immediate sensation and significance? There was so much beauty in the world, so much generosity, so much love among friends and family for life to end in extinction. Surely life could not be simply, as Macbeth put it: "a tale told by an idiot, full of sound and fury, signifying nothing"?

St. Paul explores all these themes in Romans, and argues that the only remedy for our human condition is the grace of God in Christ. Despite our failure, despite our distance from God, despite our guilt, despite the grip of death upon us, and the evil that comes from within us, St. Paul declares that because of what Christ has done for us and in us, "Therefore, there is now no condemnation for those who are in Christ Jesus, because through Christ Jesus, the law of the Spirit of life set me free from the law of sin and death," (Romans 8:1,2)

Acquitted of all charges! Rescued! Restored!

"No condemnation"! Acquitted of all charges! Set free from penal servitude! Rescued from the kingdom of darkness and restored to the realm of light in the presence of the God of love! A man may be condemned when he is guilty of a crime. A building may be condemned when it is considered dangerous. Actions may be condemned because they are reprehensible. But Christ has come to set aside such sentences. We are declared freely pardoned and fully reconciled to God.

The means of this transformation is the power of the Spirit applying the sacrifice of Christ to our life. Try as hard as we might, we cannot effect this transformation by our own efforts to be good. We need a power beyond ourselves to rescue us from our failures and their consequences: guilt, and spiritual death as separation from God. "We aren't saved from sin's grasp by knowing the commandments of God, because we can't and don't keep them, but God put into effect a different plan to save us. He sent his own Son in a human body like ours – except that ours are sinful – and destroyed sin's control over us by giving himself as a sacrifice for our sins. So now we can obey God's laws if we follow after the Holy Spirit and no longer obey the old evil nature within us." (Romans 8:3,4. *The Living Bible*)

The secret of real hope.

Romans 8 tells us about the power of the indwelling Spirit in the believer to enable us to overcome the grasp of our defective human nature. We are not condemned to live out our lives feeling defeated and despondent about our failings. The Good News, the Gospel, proclaims our Absolution and Deliverance. The chapter ends on a high note of confidence: "Who will bring any charge against those whom God has chosen? It is God who justifies. Who is he who condemns? Christ Jesus? No!" (Romans 8:33,34)

The secret of real hope is to appropriate the reality of Christ's conquering sin's control over us. Failure is not final. With the help of the Spirit who lives in us, we can experience joy and peace. Death is defeated. Access to the tree of life is restored to us. We can dwell in the house of the Lord forever.

2

THE MIND OF THE SPIRIT

"Those who live according to the sinful nature have their minds set on what that nature desires; but those who live in accordance with the Spirit have their minds set on what the Spirit desires. The mind of sinful man is death, but the mind controlled by the Spirit is life and peace; the sinful mind is hostile to God. It does not submit to God's law, nor can it do so. Those controlled by the sinful nature cannot please God.. You, however, are controlled not by the sinful nature, but by the Spirit, if the Spirit of God lives in you. And if anyone does not have the Spirit of Christ, he does not belong to Christ." (Romans 8:5-10)

William Sargant was a British psychiatrist who, in 1957, published one of the first books on the psychology of brainwashing, *Battle for the Mind.* He was heavily involved with the Intelligence Services, including the CIA Project MKULTRA. His work became termed 'The Manchurian Candidate' after the novel. His research destroyed the health, memories and lives of countless patients. He was one of the dominant figures in psychiatry in the 1970's. No one would dare to challenge him. He experimented with mind control, which had damaging effects on his patients. He believed that human beings were biological species, who resemble dogs in their brain functions. Their power of reason should not be abused by religious or political mystique that stunted reason. He saw some forms of Christianity, and particularly the effects of John Wesley's preaching, as a form of neurotic hysteria, which, however, were socially beneficial. He did not rule out that the Holy Spirit could make use of the human nervous system to strengthen faith. His aim was to reduce the mystery from God's work by explaining it in terms of biology.

None of us wants to be brainwashed or for our mind to be controlled by others, by ideologies or cults. So what do we make of what St. Paul wrote about in Romans 8:6 - "The mind controlled by the Spirit is life and peace."

Our choice in life: what we set our minds on.

Paul taught that, when our minds are receptive to the Spirit, we have access to the life in all its fullness that Jesus came to bring, and we experience peace with God, others, and within ourselves. Real hope, according to Romans 8, is to be found in living according to the Holy Spirit, and setting your mind on the things of the Spirit. Each person has a choice in life. We can set our minds on what our selfish nature desires, or what the Spirit of God desires for us. If we want a full and flourishing life, at peace with God and others, and ourselves, we will set our minds on God's purpose for us.

To set your mind on something is to make it your priority, your interest, your goal. It is what preoccupies you, what drives you, what concerns you, what occupies your time, and your energies.

The secular mind-set: tone-deaf to the spiritual.

St. Paul identifies two kinds of people. There are those who have their minds set on what their selfish nature desires. That nature is hostile to God, and rebels against any spiritual direction. It focuses upon the life of this world only. It concentrates on the visible, the seen, and has nothing at all to do with the unseen. It has nothing to do with the eternal. It excludes any reference to God. It is life lived on a purely secular plane.

This mindset may be full of ideas about improving the world. It can produce masterpieces of art and of literature and of music; but there is no God, there is no eternity, there is no Spirit. People with this mind-set are hostile to God, and do not want to be accountable to any higher authority in their personal lives. They are dead to God – alienated from God – they live as if there were no God.

Dr Martyn Lloyd-Jones writes about this mindset. "Some of your greatest moral men, some of your most cultured men in the world are in that position. They are very able, very cultured, very much interested in life. They never get drunk, they are not guilty of adultery. God is not in their thoughts, they are completely dead to God, they are living as if there were no God. That is what is meant by spiritual death. Spiritual death is to be outside the life of God…The spiritual realm does not exist for them, they scoff at it; spiritual realities mean nothing whatsoever to them; they are dead to them all. Ask them to read the New Testament, and they say that it is 'nonsense'. Draw their attention to spiritual things and they do not know what you are talking about."

"There is a well-known story which seems to me to supply a perfect illustration of this point. It concerns two great men, William Wilberforce the leader in the movement for the abolition of slavery, and William Pitt the Younger, one time Prime Minister of Britain. They were both brilliant men, they were both politicians, and they were very great friends. But William Wilberforce was converted and became a Christian, while William Pitt, like so many others, was but a formal Christian. William Wilberforce was very much concerned about his friend. He loved him as a man and was greatly concerned about his soul. He was most anxious therefore that Pitt should go with him to listen to a certain preacher, a London clergyman of the Church of England named Richard Cecil. Cecil was a great evangelical preacher, and Wilberforce delighted in his ministry, so he was ever trying to persuade Pitt to go along with him to listen to Cecil. At long last Pitt agreed to do so. Wilberforce was delighted and they went together to a service. Richard Cecil was at his best, preaching in his most spiritual and elevated manner. Wilberforce was enjoying himself, and feeling lifted up into the heavens. He could not imagine anything better, anything more enjoyable, anything more wonderful; and he was wondering what was happening to his friend William Pitt, the Prime Minister. Well, he was not left long in a state of uncertainty as to what had been happening, because, before they were even out of the building Pitt turned to Wilberforce and said, 'You know Wilberforce, I have not the slightest idea what that man has been talking about.' And he hadn't, of course. As a man can be tone deaf to music,... he was tone deaf to the spiritual. He was bored, he could not follow it, he could not understand it, he did not know what it was about. A man of great brilliance, a man of great culture, a man of great intellectual ability, but all that does not help"[1]

I had the same experience with my father, who was a business man, a man of the world, who was interested in all kinds of sports and entertainment. He came to London for my ordination, and I was anxious for him to hear my mentor, the great preacher, John Stott. My father came to the service, and when John Stott stood up to preach, promptly fell asleep. What inspired me bored him.

The spiritual mind-set

There is another kind of person. There are those who have their minds set on what the Holy Spirit desires. What does the Holy Spirit desire for us? To live by the Spirit is to keep in step with the Spirit (Galatians 4:25), to keep in tune with the Spirit. It is to seek the Spirit's direction in your life. It is to pray in the Spirit. It is to seek the will of God in your life. It is to seek the filling of the Holy Spirit, so that you may have the gifts of the Spirit to exercise your ministry. It is to work on producing the fruit of the Spirit: love, joy, peace, patience, kindness, goodness, faithfulness, gentleness, and self-control. (Galatians 4:22,23) When your mind is set on those qualities, you will experience life in all its fullness, and peace with God, peace with your neighbor, and peace

---

[1] D. Martyn Lloyd-Jones, *Romans: The Sons of God*, Zondervan: Grand Rapids, 1975, pp.9,10

within. You will enjoy an inner integration or harmony with yourself and the world.

When you have your mind set on what the Spirit desires you see the world differently. You are not dependent on the culture, or politics, or your leisure pursuits, for your happiness. You see everything you do in relationship to what God wants you to do. You know that if you are seeking God's will in your life you will be fulfilling the purpose for which you were born. You will become the highest and best you can be.

You can't do it on your own. You need the Holy Spirit to empower you.

Life is not just the survival of the fittest. You are not measured by your net worth. Your hope is in the life of the Spirit, in eternal life, not just the material world. You communicate with the unseen through the eyes of faith. You are more concerned for relationships, for helping others, for loving your neighbor, for sharing the peace you enjoy with others. You see yourself as a life-giver, bearing the life of the Spirit into every situation in which you find yourself. You want to be loving, joyful, peacemaking, patient, kind, to do good, to be faithful to others, gentle, and in control of yourself when there is reason not to be. But you know you cannot do this on your own. You need the Holy Spirit to empower you. You want to be controlled by the Spirit of Christ, not your own self-centered nature.

"Those who think they can do it on their own end up obsessed with measuring their own moral muscle but never get around to exercising it in real life. Those who trust God's action in them find that God's Spirit is in them – living and breathing God! Obsession with self in these matters is a dead end; attention to God leads us out into the open, into a spacious, free life. Focusing on the self is the opposite of focusing on God. Anyone completely absorbed in self ignores God, ends up thinking more about self than God. That person ignores who God is and what he is doing. And God isn't pleased at being ignored." (Romans 8:5-8 *The Message*)

Setting my mind on the Spirit

When I read the Bible and seek the Spirit's illumination, I am setting my mind on the Spirit. When I pray for inspiration, I am setting my mind on the Spirit. When I am seeking wisdom and direction in my life, I am setting my mind on the Spirit. When I am praying for the empowering of the Spirit so that I am to be more concerned for others than myself, I am setting my mind on the Spirit. Whenever I am praying for protection from evil for myself or my loved ones, I am setting my mind on the Spirit. When I am praying for my health, for my family, for my finances, and for our leaders, I am setting my mind on the Spirit. When I do all these things I enter more deeply into an experience of fullness of life and peace, and I have real hope.

3

THE SPIRIT OF RESURRECTION LIFE

"And if the Spirit of him who raised Jesus from the dead is living in you, he who raised Christ from the dead will also give life to your mortal bodies through his Spirit, who lives in you." (Romans 8:11)

Chuck Colson tells about celebrating Easter Sunday in Delaware in 2000. "It was a cold, windy morning, more like winter than the beginning of spring. We arrived at the Sussex Correctional Institution just as the day's first light was filtering through the morning clouds. There's always such a sense of drama about dawn on Easter morning. I invariably think about Christ's disciples hurrying to His tomb in the dark.... the sorrow, the confusion, the angels, the incredulity, the absolute, stunning thunderbolt of joy... the sun breaking through the dark clouds, the hearts on fire, and the cry that echoes down through the ages: 'Christ is risen! He is risen indeed!'

The prison, a drab, low-slung series of buildings, was opened in 1931. It holds about eleven hundred maximum-, medium-, and minimum-security inmates, all men, as well as a boot camp with one hundred beds that houses ninety men and ten women.

Franklin Graham of the Billy Graham Association, Bruce Wilkinson of Walk Thru the Bible, and I were to lead the worship services.... Our team gathered on the central area of the outdoor prison compound. We were on a raised platform, with sound equipment for the musicians, our microphones, and other paraphernalia. It was a good setup, but I was distressed when I saw the rest of the arrangement. There was a big chain-link fence between the platform and the prisoners, and fences between each section of inmates.

To make it worse it was getting colder. An icy northwest wind whipped through the prison yard. I had on a heavy, lined raincoat, and I was still chilled to the bone. My heart went out to the prisoners, who were standing in that wind with no jackets, just their thin, white, prison uniforms.

"I told the inmates my own story. I spoke about Jesus, the prisoner...."

After music by Charlie Daniels and worship teams that warmed the men up as much as anything could, I told the inmates my own story: how the risen Christ had saved me. I spoke about Jesus, the prisoner, and about what really happened at Calvary. I tried to put the story in terms that these inmates – mostly under thirty years of age – could relate to. I talked about how Jesus had been turned over to the authorities by one of His friends, who turned on Him, how He'd been held in an isolation cell, strip-searched, beaten up. I talked about the guards who gambled for His clothes, the people who just stood by staring, watching the drama unfold, the officials who cared only about their own power … and then I talked about the prisoners who hung on the crosses on either side of Jesus. One mocked Him – like the other cynics in the crowd that day. The other recognized his own sin – and the fact that Jesus really was the Son of God. And he was promised eternal life.

At that I turned the service over to Franklin Graham, who, in his clear way, took the men through the plan of salvation in the Scriptures. He invited them to receive Christ and to indicate their decision by raising their hands. Many, many men did so. *What a great Easter morning,* I thought.

But it wasn't over.

You just can't do this in prison.

Not wanting to leave out Bruce Wilkinson, I leaned over after Franklin finished and whispered to him, 'Bruce, why don't you go up and say a word to the men, and then close the service with prayer?'

He nodded and got up. I prepared to bow my head for prayer.

Bruce walked up to the microphone and looked at the inmates who were all crowded against the fence trying to get closer to the platform. They looked at him…He said, 'I want all of you men who are pushing up against the fence to move back about ten or twelve paces. …Men move back,' he said again. 'A few more steps back.' Finally the crowd of men had cleared a perimeter about twelve feet back from the fence that separated them from the podium.

'Okay,' said Bruce. 'Now I want all of the Christians, those of you who gave your lives to Christ today, those of you who have been believers for a while – I want all of you to walk forward to the fence.'

I covered my eyes with my hands. This is it. I thought. You just can't do this in prison. He's setting these guys up for trouble.

But when I looked up, to my amazement, half a dozen guys walked to the fence without hesitation. Then five or six more. They just poured forward. About two hundred inmates walked up to the fence and stood there with a kind of quiet confidence – not fidgeting, just standing and waiting, looking at Bruce.

Bruce kept pushing.

'All right,' Bruce said. 'Good. Now all you men who stepped forward… you have stepped forward as the people of God in this prison. You are the church here. And now I want you to turn around, with your backs to me. I want you to do an about-face and look at the rest of the prison population standing here.

At this point my heart was back in my mouth. The prison officials and corrections officers were shooting glances at one another, the officers watching certain inmates closely. Bruce seemed to be setting up a situation with two sets of inmates in confrontation; something like this could easily get out of hand.

But what happened was unbelievable. The Christian guys who had walked to the fence paused for a moment.

Then, almost as one, they turned around and stood looking straight into the eyes of the rest of the men.

Bruce kept pushing. 'Now,' he said, 'I want you believers to get down on your knees. You're the church in here. I'm going to pray for you. I've asked you to turn so you're facing the rest of these guys because they are your mission field. Your job as Christians is to share the gospel with them. Love them. Serve them.'

Talk about boldness! The Christian men got down on their knees, and then, without instruction, put their hands on one another's shoulders. It was such a beautiful, powerful paradox – a kneeling army of believers, arms around one another, in a posture of service before the rest of the tough, skeptical men in that institution.

"I will never forget that Easter morning in Delaware."

Bruce prayed, and a holy hush came over that cold prison yard. He prayed that these men might boldly witness to the love of Christ, that they might be filled with the grace of God, and that He would use them to build his church, extend His kingdom, so that more and more inmates in that prison community would turn their hearts to give glory to God.

After Bruce ended his prayer, he asked if any more men would like to follow Jesus Christ…and many did. Those men were still in prison, but they were free indeed.

I will never forget that Easter morning in Delaware."[1]

---

[1] Chuck Colson, *Being the Body*, W Publishing, Thomas Nelson, Nashville, 2003, pp. 32-37

What is it about the gospel of Jesus that will change the lives of even the worst of us? It is because Jesus died for our sins, and rose again from the dead to give us new life. When we open our lives to the Spirit of Jesus and follow him, God will forgive us, and give us hope for the future. This is a life-changer. St. Paul wrote about this good news in Romans 8:11.

"And if the Spirit of him who raised Jesus from the dead is living in you, he who raised Christ from the dead will also give life to your mortal bodies through his Spirit, who lives in you." (Romans 8:11, NIV)
"And if the Spirit of God, who raised up Jesus from the dead, lives in you, he will make your dying bodies live again after you die, by means of this same Holy Spirit living within you." (LB)

The life-changing Good News.

It is good news because, due to the resurrection of Jesus, we can be raised to new life in him that death can never take away. St. Paul says that there is a close connection between our resurrection and the resurrection of Christ.
"By his power God raised the Lord from the dead, and he will raise us also." (1 Cor.6:14)
"But Christ has indeed been raised from the dead, the firstfruits of those who have fallen asleep.....for as in Adam all die, so in Christ all will be made alive. But each in his own turn: Christ the firstfruits; then when he comes, those who belong to him." (1 Cor.15:20-23)

"The Lord Jesus Christ, who by the power that enables him to bring everything under his control, will transform our lowly bodies so that they may be like his glorious body." (Phil.3:21)

This is how John Stott describes this good news of the Spirit of Resurrection Life.

"The ultimate destiny of our body is not death but resurrection. Our bodies are not yet redeemed (Rom. 8:23), but they will be, and we are eagerly awaiting this event. How can we be so sure about it? Because of the nature of the indwelling Spirit. He is not only 'the Spirit of life' (Rom.8:2), but the Spirit of resurrection....Further, Christ's resurrection is the pledge and pattern of ours. The same Spirit who raised him will also raise us. The same Spirit who gives life to our spirits (Rom.8:10) will also give life to our bodies (Rom.8:11).

This life is not a prison.

This does not mean that our dead bodies will be revivified or resuscitated, and so restored to their present material existence, only to die again. No, resurrection includes transformation, the raising and changing of our body into a new and glorious vehicle of our personality, and its liberation from all frailty, disease, pain, decay and death. It is not that the spirit is to be freed from the body – as many under the influence of the Greek way of thinking, have held – but rather that the Spirit will give life to the body."[2]

---

[2] John Stott, *Romans*, InterVarsity Press: Downers Grove, 1994, pp.226,227

This gives us real hope for the future. We are not imprisoned in our bodies, to be released from it at death. We are to be given new bodies, resurrection bodies, that fits our new heavenly environment. This life is not a prison. "The critical moment for the Christian is not the moment of bodily death in hope of a blessed resurrection; it is the moment at which the man came to be in Christ. From that moment he is immortal, not, so to speak in his own right, but because Christ lives in him. When bodily death comes, it is only a matter of being 'absent from the body, present with the Lord.' The life after death is not a new life: it is the life he has been living all the time in Christ, only lived under different conditions."[3]

This is why the message of Easter is such good news. It is a message of hope for the whole world. It can change even the most hardened criminal into a saint. The Spirit gives us new life, resurrection life, beginning right now, if we invite the risen Christ to live in us.

---

[3] C.H. Dodd, *The Epistle to the Romans*, Hodder & Stoughton: London, 1932, p.126

4

EVERYTHING HAS ITS PRICE

"And if the Spirit of him who raised Jesus from the dead is living in you, he who raised Christ from the dead will also give life to your mortal bodies through his Spirit, who lives in you. Therefore, brothers, we have an obligation – but it is not to the sinful nature, to live according to it. For if you live according to the sinful nature you will die; but if by the Spirit you put to death the misdeeds of the body, you will live." (Romans 8:11-13)

If you want to be a Christian you have to be ruthless. Yes, ruthless, i.e. without pity or compassion. Are you surprised I would say that? I don't mean without pity and compassion for those who deserve it, but to be ruthless with your sinful nature. We are to be prepared to put to death the misdeeds of the body i.e. to eliminate, to kill, the temptations to sin in our lives. If you aren't prepared to do that you cannot live according to the Spirit of Christ. Just as addictions can cause physical death, e.g. smoking; sin can cause spiritual death. In the season of Lent I give up something to remind myself of the need to be free of having to eat or drink or do something. Lent always begins with a call to self-examination and repentance; prayer, fasting and self-denial; and we read the account of the temptations of Jesus during his forty days in the wilderness. It is a reality check, a douche of cold water, to wake us up to the hard facts of life – everything has its price. If you want to go along with the temptations of the world, the flesh and the devil, you have to accept the consequences – a life on the dark side – as opposed to the light and love of God - a life with all the sickness that darkness entails. If you want to live in the light, and fulfill your God-given potential and become all that you are created and redeemed to be, then you have to stand, fight and kill the temptation to be otherwise. There can be no compromise or neutrality. Life in all its fullness and wholeness, what the Bible calls holiness, has its price.

Self-Discipline

The Christian life requires self-discipline. "Endure hardship with us like a good soldier of Christ Jesus. No one serving as a soldier gets involved in civilian affairs – he wants to please his commanding officer." (2 Timothy 2:3,4)

The follower of Christ has been given the gift of the indwelling Holy Spirit to enable him to overcome temptation. We are empowered by the Spirit when we set our minds on the things of the Spirit. The Spirit enables us to exercise our will to resist temptation. Our natural bodies, with their sinful tendencies, are still going to want to be indulged. This doesn't mean that followers of Christ are to be killjoys, who cannot have fun. But it does mean that there are moral boundaries, and virtues to be respected if we are to be authentic and faithful.

The popularity of self-indulgence.

A belief that is popular today is that we should not deny the desires of our bodies. If you want a sexual relationship with a person, whether they be married or single, of your gender or not, then indulge yourself. If you feel that your personal identity is constrained by your biology, then change your gender. If you feel that you deserve the same rights and privileges as those who have committed themselves to marriage and family, then, sue for it in a court of law. If others disagree with you on the basis of their faith and morals then accuse them of hatred and make it a civil rights issue. If you feel that your sense of self-worth demands multi-million dollar compensation packages, then negotiate for it. If you need to be pampered and waited on, and agreed with, in order to feel good about yourself, then surround yourself with those who will indulge you. If you are obsessed with your own health problems to the exclusion of being interested in the problems of others, then dominate the conversation by indulging your preoccupations and anxieties. If your need to feel important requires you to be right on every issue then impose your opinions on others and never listen respectfully to a contrary opinion. Indulge yourself. Make yourself the center of attention. But the Bible teaches that just because we want something to feel good, or don't feel like doing something we should, does not mean that we should indulge ourselves. The Gospel is counter-cultural. True freedom results from not being a slave to your selfish desires.

The price of success.

Paul uses the analogy of the athlete. (1 Corinthians 9:24-27) If you want to be successful it has its price – you have to go into training. You have to deny yourself indulgences, and enter into a strict regimen if you want to be your best. "I beat my body and make it my slave so that after I have preached to others, I myself will not be disqualified for the prize." Now this sounds like radical language. It is the language of discipline and self-denial. Paul calls it "putting to death the misdeeds of the body". Give no quarter to the temptation to natural indulgence of our bodily desires for comfort and pleasure.

Jesus goes even further in the Sermon on the Mount (Matthew 5:27-30). He teaches us to metaphorically amputate that part of our body that causes us to sin. It is better to lose one part of our body than to allow it to make you go to hell. In other words, if proximity to the source of temptation leads you into sin, then don't go there. For example, if watching certain kinds of movies, or television shows, results in your imagination being filled with unworthy and depraved thoughts, then don't watch them, don't look. This is a real problem today because of the availability of so much pornography and violence on the internet and television. People have become addicted to voyeurism. Instead of avoidance of these sources of temptation they are indulging them. Paul said that we must kill, mortify, not indulge these temptations.

That this teaching of self-denial of the sinful desires of the body – mortification - is relevant to our culture today is seen in the moral relativism that is rampant in our society. Because we are all sinners, and all human, it even surfaces in the church. Pastors who preach one thing and are found to do differently bring embarrassment upon their congregations. When they indulge in flamboyant and luxurious lifestyles they mock the Jesus whom they claim to serve. When they think that they are special and deserve their immoral pleasures, and that the rules don't apply to them, they are blind to their sinfulness.

The social consequences of our actions.

Ted Haggard, pastor of New Life Church in Colorado Springs for twenty years, and president of the National Association of Evangelicals, in November 2006 was caught in a sex-and-drugs scandal involving a male prostitute in Denver. Patton Dodd, who was on the staff of New Life Church for eight years has written, "One of his most legendary sermons was titled, 'There's No Such Thing as a Secret.' Truth will out, preached Haggard, so you might as well confess your darkest impulses and actions. Haggard's double life was a searing revelation to his family, his church, and his closest friends. Another legendary Haggard sermon was called, 'How Much Is Your Sin Going To Cost Me?' It was the pastor's sly, wry way of reminding us that there are social consequences for our actions. When we lie, cheat, and steal, we incur debts of time, emotion, and material treasure that our family and friends have to pay. Have integrity, he said, so that no one has to clean up after your mistakes."

The illusion of a perfect life.

HBO premiered *The Trials of Ted Haggard*, a documentary by Alexandra Pelosi that followed the ex-minister through the dreary months following his fall. Dodd wrote, "The other night, I watched Pelosi's documentary with several friends who had experienced Haggard's downfall together. Afterward, we reflected on one of the benevolent outcomes of the tragedy: It forced us to deal in reality. Haggard had crafted the illusion of a perfect life. He rarely showed personal weakness, and he preached that faith in God and a can-do attitude guaranteed a life of happiness. Something always does – and always did – smell off about the 'Jesus makes life perfect' version of Christian witness. It's not consistent with the Bible's record of pain and suffering, much less than what we know of ourselves. But hey, it sure seemed to be working for Haggard. His smile was constant, his energy endless. His life was an argument for the power of positive thinking."

A Clarion Call to Personal Honesty

"Haggard's downfall was a clarion call to personal honesty. It challenged us to do the gritty work of growing in self-knowledge. John Calvin, echoing Augustine, wrote that there is 'no deep knowing of God without a deep knowing of self.' Self-knowledge is, or should be, a natural outcome of a proper Christian life, because confession is a core discipline. The Christian is invited to admit the full truth of his or her life – as our Scripture has it, to 'walk in the light.' Christianity should be a path of self-disclosure. There is no such thing as a secret."

This problem is not just confined to sexual sin, or to preachers. It is common to all men and women who think they have got it all together, and are self-satisfied and self-righteous. Unfortunately, the failure to face the reality of our temptations to indulge ourselves, results in continued self-deception. We justify our self-indulgence. We make excuses for ourselves. We capitulate to our desires. As unpalatable as he may seem, St. Paul is the realist about human nature. Our only real hope is, not to give in, but to fight and defeat our temptations in the power of the Spirit. It is easier to give in to temptation, but it has its price. Real hope comes from putting to death our temptations to sin and so deprive our self-indulgent desires of their power to control us. That is the way to victory, life and peace.

5

LED BY THE SPIRIT

"Those who are led by the Spirit of God are sons of God." (Romans 8:14)

It is not fun to be lost. When I don't know where I am I can panic. My heart starts to race and I begin to perspire. It is not until I find my bearings that I calm down. Real hope comes from knowing that you are being guided by the Spirit in your life's journey, and that you can never become lost. If you know that you are walking with Christ, and therefore going in the right direction, you can have confidence and assurance about the future. If you feel that the Spirit of God is leading you to progress or mature in holiness and making you into a better person, then you can handle suffering, setbacks and challenges. If you know that God is in front of you, leading the way every day, as you make decisions and seek guidance, you feel secure and safe. If danger lurks all around you, and you fear the future as you attempt to navigate through the minefield of your present circumstances, but you believe that the Spirit of Christ is leading you, you will have the courage to continue on. Not to be led by the Spirit is to be without a chart or compass on your journey. Not to be led by the Spirit is to be lost.

The Christian believes that in this life we are on a journey, a pilgrimage, and that we are being led by God the Holy Spirit. Despite all the obstacles and trials on the journey, all the temptations to turn aside, or to quit the journey, we believe God is leading us on to the Promised Land. On the way we have much to learn about following the Spirit, about being willing to be led by the Spirit.

The persuasion of the Spirit

How does this take place? It is not a passive or negative description, such as being led astray, or being led by the nose. Neither is it being 'forced' or 'driven.' The Spirit does not drive the children of God. Instead the Spirit persuades us. He leads us by persuasion; not by brute force, not against our will. He persuades the will, which is a very different thing. What the Spirit does is to enlighten and persuade us so that we desire to follow God's will in our lives. The Spirit puts a new principle, a new disposition into us, and then we desire the things of God.

Consider Isaiah 30:21: "Whether you turn to the right or to the left, your ears will hear a voice behind you, saying, 'This is the way; walk in it.'" We hear and respond. That is how God guides – by his Word, by the persuasion of the Holy Scriptures.

To be 'led by the Spirit' means that our life is guided and determined and directed by the Holy Spirit. That is what makes a Christian a child of God. The natural man is neither guided by the Spirit nor led by the Spirit. He is guided by his own desires; he feels an urge to do something, and he indulges it. He is guided by his impulses, instincts, passions, by all that his physical life in its separation from God desires. He might be guided by the mind of the world, the culture, the morés of the social group, as are those who do not think for themselves. They do what everyone else does. They are led and guided by the powers that control the media. Some are led by their reason. But natural human reason is not enough. Human understanding is defective. The natural man does not see the subtleties of his situation. He is at best guided by reason and common sense; never anything higher than that. He is not led by the Spirit; he uses his own understanding, his will-power and his own determination. Jesus called such people children of the devil: "You belong to your father, the devil, and you want to carry out your father's desire." (John 8:44)

The guidance of the Spirit

The follower of Christ is in an entirely different position and category. He is not led by his own natural powers, but, ultimately, by the Spirit of God. The Spirit of God may lead him partly through his reason and in other ways, but what is central about him is that he and his life seek to be governed by the leading, the direction, of the Holy Spirit of God. That does not mean for a moment that he is perfect. He is not perfect. But it can be said of him that the main and obvious tendency and direction of his life is that which is guided by the Holy Spirit.

We can test what we believe is the leading of the Holy Spirit in our lives. The truth which the Holy Spirit conveys to us is the truth which is written in the Spirit-inspired Scriptures. The Spirit leads us into a new way of Christ-like living through the teaching of the Bible. The Holy Spirit leads us to a knowledge and understanding of the truth about Jesus Christ, His Person and His Work. The Holy Spirit leads us into an understanding of the whole purpose of God in the world. The Holy Spirit leads us to believe that God has a great plan and purpose for the world, that he is going to bring to fulfillment.

Can you say that your life, taken as a whole – your thought life, your feelings, your actions, your will, seeks to be under the direction of the Spirit of God? Can you say this: 'With all my faults and failures, and all that is true of me, I can say that I want the directing force and principle in my life to be the Spirit of God?' St. Paul states that if you can say that, you are a son or daughter of God. Is the main direction of your life following the leading of the Spirit of God? Is it your greatest desire that it should be? If it is, whatever else may be true of you, whatever your faults and failures, you are a 'child of God.'

God is educating, training you

With that designation, being adopted into God's family you have a similarity of mind and of outlook. You look at everything from God's standpoint, from the aspect of eternity. God looks at you in a very special way, as his beloved sons and daughters. He takes a very special interest in you, in your well-being, in your welfare, in your good. He is interested in every one of you individually. You may not think that to be true from time to time when you are in trouble. Sometimes he may have to discipline you as a loving Father, so that you will learn and mature.

" 'My dear child, don't shrug off God's discipline, but don't be crushed by it either. It's the child he loves that he disciplines, the child he embraces, he also corrects.' God is educating you, that's why you must never drop out. He's treating you as dear children. This trouble you're in isn't punishment; it's *training*, the normal experience of children. Only irresponsible parents leave children to fend for themselves. Would you prefer an irresponsible God? We respect our own parents for training and not spoiling us, so why not embrace God's training so we can truly *live*? While we were children, our parents did what *seemed* best to them. But God is doing what is best for us, training us to live God's holy best. At the time, discipline isn't much fun. It always feels like it's going against the grain. Later, of course, It pays off handsomely, for it's the well-trained who find themselves mature in their relationships with God." (Hebrews 12:5-10, *The Message*)

The correction of God

Being led by the Spirit is a sign that we are children of God. Sometimes that leading involves being corrected in love. Experiencing correction can be painful. We are tempted to believe that God doesn't love us. But correction has a purpose. We learn the errors of our ways. We learn what is good and what is not. We learn to follow God's leading, and to do what is best.

If you feel that you are in a correction phase of life, because of some suffering you are experiencing; whether it be due to finances, or health, or relationships, then seek the leading of the Spirit, and be assured that your suffering proves that you are a beloved child of God. "The trouble you're in isn't punishment... God is doing what is best for you, training us to live God's holy best." Let the Spirit lead you safely through this minefield, to the other side.[1]

As I look back on my life I see how the Spirit has led me and corrected me from one stage to another. Trained me me under the instruction of a godly pastor, Harvey Teulon, and his associate, Graham Lamont, in my youth. Led me to go to England for my theological education. Led me to All Souls Church, Langham Place, London, and the mentoring of John Stott as I began my ministry. Led me to meet my wife, Antoinette, who has been the greatest civilizing influence on my life. Through her the Spirit led me to the USA and Gordon College, Massachusetts, and the privilege of working with Harold Ockenga. Each stage has had its challenges and growing pains. But in all the Spirit led and therefore I believe is still leading me. What I see so clearly retrospectively is an encouragement for the present and future leading I can anticipate. God's leading and correction is training me for the life to come.

[1] Some material in this chapter comes from D. Martyn Lloyd-Jones, *Romans: The Sons of God*, pp. 159ff.

6

DELIVERANCE FROM FEAR

"For you did not receive a spirit that makes you a slave again to fear, but you have received the spirit of sonship. And by him we cry, 'Abba, Father.'" (Romans 8:15)

Fear – what image does that word conjure up in your mind? Is it debilitating disease, or financial insolvency, or worries about your children or grandchildren, or the unknown future, or an unforeseen accident, or being abandoned, or the unpredictable, or separation from God - hell? What is it that wakes you up in the night? What is it that occasions a black cloud of depression to settle over you? Peggy Noonan wrote in the *Wall Street Journal* on February 20, 2009: "This isn't like the stock market crash of 1987 or the collapse of the dot-com bubble in 2001. People are not feeling passing anger or disappointment, they're feeling truly frightened." Writing again, in March 14, 2009, under the heading: *There's No Pill for This Kind of Depression*, she wrote, "I spoke to a

Manhattan-based psychiatrist who said there is an uptick in the number of his patients reporting depression and anxiety. He believes part of the reason is that we're in a new place, that 'When people move into a new home they increasingly recognize the importance of their previous environment.' Our new home is post-prosperity America; the old one was the abundance; we miss it. But he also detected a political dimension to his patient's anguish. He felt that many see our leaders as 'selfish and dishonest,' that 'our institutions have been revealed as incompetent and undependable.' People feel 'unled, overwhelmed,' the situation 'seemingly unsalvageable.' The net result? He thinks what he is seeing, within and without his practice, is a 'psychological pandemic of fear' as to the future of things – of our country, and even of mankind."

Battling fear

Are you experiencing any of these things? Fear, anxiety attacks, depression, are common maladies in our world. We are supposed to be on top of things all the time, but the reality is that most of us fight fear, worry and depression. We need all the help we can get to battle an attitude of fear.

How do you deal with your fears? St. Paul addresses this problem with the following promises in Romans 8:15 -
"For you did not receive a spirit that makes you a slave again to fear, but you received the Spirit of sonship. And by him we cry, 'Abba, Father'." (NIV) "Nor are you meant to relapse into the old slavish attitude of fear-you have been adopted into the very family circle of God and you can say

with a full heart, 'Father, my Father.'" (J.B. Phillips) "And so we should not be like cringing, fearful slaves, but we should behave like God's very own children, adopted into the bosom of his family, and calling to him, 'Father, Father.'" (Living Bible)

"No fear"

Before faith in Christ, we were subject to slavery to fear. We feared death, we feared judgment, we feared suffering, we feared guilt, we feared the bad opinion of others, we feared failure, we feared rejection. When we met Christ we heard him say: "Fear not." He conquered fear with imperturbable faith. (cf. The Miracle of the Stilling of the Storm - Mark 4:35-39). The message of the angels at Bethlehem and at the Empty Tomb was: "Fear Not!" The vision of Christ to John in Revelation 1:17 was "Do not be afraid. I am the First and the Last. I am the Living One; I was dead, and behold I am alive for ever and ever! And I hold the keys of death and Hades."

To be enslaved to something is to be controlled by it. When fear takes over we are paralyzed. Paul tells us that we received from God, not a spirit of fear, but a Spirit of Sonship. Instead of being controlled by a spirit of fear, we are meant to be liberated by the Spirit of Sonship. Because of what Christ has done on our behalf on the Cross, we are freed from fear to enjoy life in a personal, loving, intimate relationship with God our Father, *Abba*! The term Paul used, *Abba*, is familiar. It is a child's word for his father, Papa. It is the word Jesus used in the garden of Gethsemane. "*Abba*, Father, everything is possible for you. Take this cup from me. Yet not what I will, but what you will." (Mark 14:36) He trusted in his Father to do what was best. He accepted what had to be. He surrendered to his Father's will because he knew his Father loved him and would only do what was best.

Crying for Papa

This is not a purely intellectual assent to the truth of our relationship with God. The Spirit whom we receive, when we receive Christ into our lives, warms our hearts, our affections, for God. By this Spirit of sonship we ***cry***, "Abba, Father.' '***Cry***' denotes strong emotion. It expresses fervency, earnestness, importunity. It signifies a real knowledge and intimate relationship with God. It is a cry expecting a response. It is a call for help from One whom we can rely upon to answer. It is not an academic exercise of contacting a distant and aloof God. This is a communication with someone we know.

This spirit of sonship is especially treasured by those who never experienced a close relationship with their earthly fathers. Many of us grew up in families where there was little closeness and much emotional absence. My father was a good, hard-working man, popular with his peers, attractive, an accomplished golfer, but he and I were never close. I got the impression that he did not want to spend much time with me. When my relationship with God became important to me it met a need for affirmation and acceptance that I was feeling. I experienced a love that was new to me. It gave me a confidence that overcame my adolescent insecurities.

This relationship with the Father was made possible by Jesus. It was Jesus who made God known to me in this intimate way. It was Jesus who broke down the barrier of sin between myself and God. He is the Way, the Truth, and the Life, "No one comes to the Father except through me." (John 14:6) We only know God in this intimate way through how Jesus modeled his own relationship with his Father. Only the Son could show us God as Father.

The uniqueness of Christianity is that it proclaims a personal relationship with God. To know that God is your loving, heavenly Father, and that you can cry out to him for help when a spirit of fear attempts to enslave you, is to realize that you have received the Spirit of Sonship. Our heavenly Father can break the power of the spirit of fear if we are able to trust in him, and to surrender to him, as Jesus did in the garden of Gethsemane, or in the boat on the lake. Yet, even devout Christians can go through periods of fear and depression.

The emotional illnesses of William Cowper

William Cowper, the author of many hymns and a noted poet in the 18th century was depressed first at the age of 21, and from time to time thereafter for the next ten years. At 31 he had his first catastrophic psychotic breakdown, and at the time of his recovery he committed his life to Christ. He was to have four more depressive illnesses before he died at 68. In between these times he was amazingly productive as a letter-writer and a poet.

He had terrible dreams and hallucinations. In the middle of these nocturnal terrors he came to the insane conclusion that God had commanded him to take his own life. His attempted suicide failed and he descended into a downward spiral of tragic depression and despair. He eventually improved but remained a recluse, rarely venturing into society. Yet, despite his illness, he settled down to a calm and contented routine of reading, writing, and gardening. Some of his most famous poetry was produced in his later life. In 1773 he wrote a hymn that expressed the challenge of how to understand times of hardship, fear and anxiety.

God moves in a mysterious way
His wonders to perform;
He plants his footsteps in the sea,
And rides upon the storm.

Deep in unfathomable mines
Of never-failing skill
He treasures up his bright designs,
And works his sovereign will.

Ye fearful saints, fresh courage take;
The clouds ye so much dread
Are big with mercy, and shall break
In blessings on your head.

Judge not the Lord by feeble sense,
But trust him for his grace;
Behind a frowning providence
He hides a smiling face.

Blind unbelief is sure to err,
And scan his work in vain;
God is his own interpreter,
And he will make it plain.

When we don't know why we are going through a hard time we are discouraged, anxious and fearful. Cowper, out of his own painful experience, gives a way of coping. He believed that God was working out his mysterious purpose. God uses the storms of life, the clouds and darkness, to eventually bless us.

Kathryn Greene-McCreight has written about her affliction of bipolar disorder in *Darkness Is My Only Companion: A Christian Response to Mental Illness* (Brazos Press, Grand Rapids 2006). Anyone who is similarly afflicted, and their loved ones, would do well to benefit from her experience and insights.

We cannot always see what God is doing in our circumstances. We must trust God for his grace, and that one day he will make it all plain to us. In the meantime he gives us real hope through these promises and the witness of those who share the spirit of sonship with us.

7

THE WITNESS OF THE SPIRIT

"The Spirit himself testifies with our spirit that we are God's children." (Romans 8:16)

David Whyte wrote in a poem entitled, *SELF PORTRAIT*

> I want to know if you belong or feel abandoned,
> if you can know despair or see it in others.
> I want to know if you are prepared to live in the world
> with its harsh need
> to change you. If you can look back
> with firm eyes,
> saying this is where I stand.[1]

"I want to know if you belong or feel abandoned." The need to belong is strong in us. We want to feel valued, not abandoned. We want to feel loved, not unloved. We long for

---

[1] David Whyte, *River Flow*, Many Rivers Press, Langley, Washington, 2007, p.347

a sense of identity that gives us worth. We search for it in all kinds of places – in our work, in our families, in our children, in our friendships, in our creativity, in our achievements, in our wealth.

Who Am I?

Who am I? is one of the basic questions of life. We find our identity in our roles: as a wife or husband, as a mother or father, and when the children leave home there can be an identity crisis if the marriage has been neglected for the children. For some, it is only when the grandchildren arrive that a new sense of identity is fulfilled.

Or it may be our school associations that give us an identity – our basketball or football teams. For many it is their work, their careers, their service on boards, their volunteer work, that give them an identity. We gain a sense of belonging to a group that values our contribution. When we age, and we are sought out no longer to serve on boards, or associations, we experience a diminution of worth. Nobody seems to want us. We feel abandoned and not appreciated. People don't know our achievements. We get depressed because we feel the loss of identity. But maybe we have been seeking for our identity in the wrong places.

All earthly roles eventually pass away. All jobs come to an end. One definition of sin is the despairing refusal to find your deepest identity in your relationship and service to God. "Sin is seeking to become oneself, to get an identity, apart from God."[2] Our need for worth is so powerful that

---

[2] Tim Keller, *The Reason for God*, 162

whatever we base our identity and value on we essentially 'deify;' even when it is good, such as family.

What do you want to know about your identity – who you are? To whom do you belong that will last and give you a stable and enduring sense of worth?

St. Paul addresses this need in Romans 8. He wants to assure us about God's provision for us. He wants us to know that we belong to God, that God does not abandon us – that nothing can separate us from the love of God that is in Christ (8:39), if we are trusting in him.

Acceptance and security

The Spirit has a special role to play in that reassurance. "The Spirit himself testifies with our spirit that we are God's children." The Spirit gives an absolute certainty and assurance of our loving and intimate relationship to God. The image is that of an expert witness in a trial. This witness can be relied upon because of his particular expertise. The Spirit should know about the nature of our relationship with God, since this is the Spirit of God who testifies about our belonging to God.

This is a theme in Paul's writings. He uses different images to convey the same truth, e.g. the *sealing* and the *deposit* of the Spirit.

"Now it is God who makes both us and you stand firm in Christ. He anointed us, set his seal of ownership on us, and put his Spirit in our hearts as a deposit, guaranteeing what is to come." (2 Cor.1:21,22)

"Having believed, you were marked in Christ with a seal, the promised Holy Spirit, who is a deposit, guaranteeing our inheritance." (Eph.1:13,14)

The sealing of the Spirit is that which assures me that I am a child of God, and therefore an heir of God. A seal is a sign of belonging. The Holy Spirit identifies us as belonging to Jesus, just as the seal on a letter or the stamp on a sheep identifies its ownership. Baptism is the outward sign of the seal of the Spirit, by which we are marked as Christ's own forever.

The deposit of the Spirit gives me an installment of my inheritance, a first down-payment of what I am later to receive in its fullness. The Spirit assures us of our inheritance in the future. He gives us a pledge of the fuller life that is to come. The word is used of an engagement ring – the promise of love that makes a commitment to us of life together.

Assurance of the Spirit

The Spirit, by a direct operation on our minds and hearts and spirits gives us an absolute certainty and assurance that we are God's children. God gives us an overwhelming convincing experience of the indwelling Spirit so that we will have confidence about God's unending love for us. There may be suffering and doubts in this life, for the relationship is not yet consummated. We live between the engagement and the wedding, between the promise and the hope, between the present experience of love and the future realization of it. Yet despite questioning and the pain of this life, the Spirit gives us a testimony, a witness, that we can trust, that we can rely upon, that we belong to God even when we feel abandoned.

How does the Spirit give us this witness, this testimony? Dr. Martyn Lloyd-Jones writes:

"How does it come? Sometimes it comes when a Christian is alone, reading the Scriptures quietly; perhaps reading a passage which he has read many times before. Suddenly the passage seems to come out of the Book and speak to him directly in this particular way. It does not give him some general knowledge, but it stands out and meets him, and impresses on his mind and heart and spirit in an unmistakable manner this personal message. It is as if it were written only for him, that he is a child of God. That is the commonest way in which it comes – through a word or a passage of Scripture. Sometimes this experience happens to a man when he is not reading. Suddenly a word of Scripture that he has read before is brought into his mind . He is not thinking about it – he may actually be thinking about something quite different – but suddenly it is impressed upon his inner mind, and he becomes convinced that God loves him, and that he is a child of God. The Spirit takes a word and brings it to him and impresses it upon him in an absolutely unmistakable manner. It may happen in a religious service....The preacher says something which means nothing to the vast majority of the people, but to one soul that had been unhappy, uncertain and doubting, and attacked by the devil, it is the very voice of God speaking and telling him that he is a child of God, and that God loves him (or her) in particular. But this assurance does not always come through the Scripture. It has happened to many without any words at all; it is just an inner consciousness in the spirit given by the Spirit of God himself, apart from Scripture."[3]

Many great men and women have recorded their experience of the witness of the Spirit in their spirit. Sarah

---

[3] D. Martyn Lloyd-Jones, *Romans, the Sons of God*, Zondervan, Grand Rapids, 1975, p.306f.

Edwards, the wife of Jonathan Edwards, president of Princeton, was distinguished by her graceful and expressive features, her vigorous mind, fine culture, and fervent piety. She wrote about what happened to her in 1742:

Sarah Edwards - Witness of the Spirit

"I cannot find language to express how certain [the everlasting love of God] appeared, the everlasting mountains and hills were but shadows to it. My safety and happiness and eternal enjoyment of God's immutable love, seemed as durable and unchangeable as God himself. The presence of God was so near and so real that I seemed scarcely conscious of anything else. All night I continued in a constant, clear and lively sense of the heavenly sweetness of Christ's excellent and transcendent love, of his nearness to me and of my nearness to Him with an inexpressibly sweet calmness of soul in an entire rest in him. I think that what I felt each minute during the continuance of the whole time was worth more than all the outward comfort and pleasure which I had enjoyed in my whole life put together. This exaltation of soul subsided into a heavenly calm and rest of soul in God which was even sweeter than what preceded it." [4]

---

[4] D. Martyn Lloyd-Jones, op.cit., p.347

Seek the witness of the Spirit in your life. Seek the assurance which the Spirit wants you to enjoy. God offers you this witness, this sealing, this deposit of the Spirit. By receiving this witness you are assured of belonging to God as his child. The Spirit testifies with your spirit that you are God's children. Jesus promised: "Which of you fathers, if your son asks for a fish, will give him a snake instead? Or if he asks for an egg will give him a scorpion? If you then, though you are evil, know how to give good gifts to your children, how much more will your Father in heaven give the Holy Spirit to those who ask him?" (Luke 11:11-13)

8

HEIRS OF GOD

"Now if we are children, then we are heirs – heirs of God." (Romans 8:17)

1997 was going to be an expensive year! My younger daughter, Amelia, was to be married in Dallas on January 21, and my older daughter, Carrie, decided to get married in San Antonio on March 22. Two weddings in three months were to be quite a challenge for my finances. My mother had died in June 1996. My father had predeceased her eight years earlier. Four months later, there was an envelope in the mail from my parent's executor enclosing a check in settlement of their estate. My inheritance had arrived! Modest as it was, it paid for the weddings, enabled me to pay off some debt, and took care of some other needs. To be an heir and to be the beneficiary of an inheritance, no matter how small, is worth celebrating. St. Paul recognized that when he wrote:
"The Spirit himself testifies with our spirit that we are God's children. Now if we are children, then we are heirs – heirs of God…" (Romans 8:16,17)

Those who are led by the Spirit of God are the children of God (Rom.8:14) Those who are open to the Spirit of Christ, and receive him into their hearts, become children of God, and heirs of God. Remember what John says about the coming of Jesus into this world from eternity. "He was in the world, and though the world was made through him, the world did not recognize him. He came to that which was his own, but his own did not receive him. Yet all who received him, to those who believed in his name, he gave the right to become children of God – children born not of natural descent, nor of human decision or a husband's will, but born of God." (John 1:10-13) All who receive Christ into their lives and believe in him as their Savior and Lord, are given the power, the right, the authority, to regard themselves as children of God.

Not guests but family

Therefore, we are not to be strangers to God, alienated from God, enemies of God, but his beloved children. "Consequently, you are no longer foreigners and aliens, but fellow citizens, with God's people and members of God's household, built on the foundation of the apostles and prophets, with Christ Jesus himself as the chief cornerstone." (Ephesians 2:19,20) We are not guests in God's house, but family. We live with God, eat at his Table, and learn at his feet, by listening to his Word. God's house is our home.

But we are more than just any children of God. We are also heirs of God. God has a great inheritance in store for us. He mentions our inheritance because we need encouragement in this life. In this life we share in the sufferings of Christ. We can be tempted to believe that God does not love us. But we are assured that we share in the sufferings of Christ in order that we may share in his glory. That glory is in the future. It is not in this life. "In this world," said Jesus, "you will have trouble. But take heart! I have overcome the world." (John 16:33)

Not a panacea for this world's ills

There is a tendency in some Christian circles to promise more for this life than is warranted by the Scriptures. Some preachers and teachers give the impression that if you receive Jesus and walk faithfully in his Way that you will find all your problems solved in this life. This was not true for Jesus or his apostles. They suffered and died. They were persecuted and executed. Christianity is not a panacea for this world's ills. But the Gospel gives you the comfort and strength to endure suffering. It gives you real hope for the future. The inheritance of God is a promise to be fulfilled. The "present sufferings are not worth comparing with the glory that will be revealed in us." (Romans 8:18) The inheritance is guaranteed by the Spirit. It is gold-plated and secure.

This divine inheritance is the theme of the Bible from the beginning. The promise of a great inheritance was first made to Abraham and his descendants. "All these people were still living by faith when they died. They did not receive the things promised; they only saw them and welcomed them from a distance. And they admitted that they were strangers and aliens on earth....they were longing for a better country – a heavenly one." (Hebrews 11:13-16) God's people were looking for the fulfillment of the promised inheritance. Things went wrong for them, they suffered greatly, but they never lost hope, because of the promise of the coming Messiah who would bring deliverance.

We are God's people, God's children, God's heirs, who have hope in God fulfilling his purposes and promises. God has a plan, not only for this world, for this mortal life, but also for eternity, for a new heaven and a new earth. We are part of that plan for the future.

What would it be like to live in this world, with all its suffering, with all the troubles people have to endure, and not to have hope, to feel that there is nothing to look forward to? That is the condition of many people. They have lost hope, and they despair of ever achieving any happiness. That is why the Gospel is so important. That is why God commissions us to share his Good News with others. That is why our personal witness to the promises of God may be the only way others may hear of them.

Our inheritance

What is the divine inheritance we may look forward to? Jesus describes a picture of the Son of Man coming at the end of the age and sitting upon the throne of his glory: "All the nations will be gathered before him, and he will separate the people one from another as a shepherd separates the sheep from the goats. He will put the sheep on his right and the goats on his left. Then the King will say to those on his right, 'Come, you who are blessed by my Father; take your inheritance, the kingdom prepared for you since the creation of the world.'" (Matthew 25:31-34)

That is the promise! That is what we can look forward to: 'the kingdom prepared for you since the creation of the world.' That is the same way it is described by the Lord to Saul of Tarsus when he was converted on the road to Damascus and commissioned to preach the Gospel. "I am going to send you to the Gentiles to open their eyes to their true condition so that they may repent and live in the light of God instead of in Satan's darkness, so that they may receive forgiveness for their sins and God's inheritance along with all people everywhere whose sins are cleansed away, who are set apart by faith in me." (Acts 26:17,18 LB) When Paul prays in Ephesians he prays that "the eyes of your heart may be enlightened in order that you may know the hope to which he has called you, the riches of his glorious inheritance in the saints." (1:18)

Our birthright and destiny

The New Testament does not concentrate on this life and this world, but on that which is to come. Believers in Christ are described as heirs of salvation. Peter tells us that we have been given a "new birth into a living hope through the resurrection of Jesus Christ from the dead, and into an inheritance that can never perish, spoil or fade kept in heaven for you." (1 Peter 1:3,4)

This hope of God's inheritance is the great promise of the Scriptures from the beginning to the end. It is the hallmark of the Christian, that we keep our eyes upon our inheritance as children of God. This is our birthright, our destiny.

Is this your habitual way of thinking of yourself? Do you live rejoicing day by day in the fact that you are a child of God, and because a child, then an heir? What is your heart set upon: the things of this world, or the things of the world to come? This present world passes away. What we take with us is only what God gives us to inherit – his kingdom. Therefore we should seek first his kingdom and his righteousness. We should discover in this life all that we can about the kingdom of God which we will inherit. We can look forward, and wait, and be comforted and encouraged by this hope, of the great inheritance which will one day be ours to enjoy.[1]

---

[1] Includes some material from D. Martyn Lloyd-Jones, *Romans, The Sons of God*, pp.400-411

9

CO-HEIRS WITH CHRIST

"Now if we are children, then we are heirs – heirs of God and co-heirs with Christ." (Romans 8:17)

The Wall Street Journal (April 22, 2009), under the heading: *"Dogs Get Small Bite of Helmsley Grants*", reports that the trustees for the estate of Leona Helmsley announced $136 million in charitable gifts, using their court-sanctioned authority to override her wishes for her money to be spent on behalf of dogs. The trustees went to court to determine their discretion in giving the money away, arguing that the will didn't exclude other charitable pursuits. Most of the grants went to medical research causes. Others went to homeless shelters, food banks and emergency-services programs in New York. Only $1 million, went to dog-related causes such as the ASPCA. Mrs Helmsley's fortune had been estimated at $5-8 billion after her death at age 87 in 2007. It all goes to show that no matter how hard we try, we cannot completely control our money after we die.

Life is a matter of receiving and releasing. We receive what we are given by our parents, teachers and mentors, and we release to our children, and other heirs, what we have acquired. As we age, we have to decide what to do with what we have. We have to plan to distribute our estate. Sometimes we resent having to do so.

"I hated all the things I toiled for under the sun, because I must leave them to the one who comes after me. And who knows whether he will be a wise man or a fool? Yet he will have control over all the work into which I have poured my effort and skill under the sun. For a man may do all his work with wisdom, knowledge and skill, and then he must leave all he owns to someone who has not worked for it." (Ecclesiastes 2:18-21)

Who is going to inherit the family heirlooms? Who will appreciate the china, the silver, the paintings, that special collection, the furniture, the books, and the rugs? Who will appreciate our memory, all that we have done, all that we have stood for and believed in?

Some, like Leona Helmsley, leave their estate to their pets. But whoever we are we must release what we have, and be reborn into a new life. "For we brought nothing into the world, and we can take nothing out of it." (1 Timothy 6:6) Aging requires relinquishing what we have as our world contracts, until all we have is our basic necessities. It is only when we have nothing that we appreciate what we are given. God's plan for us is that we will receive our enduring inheritance in the life to come. We are to look forward to eternal life as a child of God, and receive what God has in store for us in his kingdom. Beyond this lifetime our world expands again to include all that God bestows on those who love him.

"Now if we are children, then we are heirs – heirs of God and co-heirs with Christ." (Romans 8:17 NIV) "For all God gives to his Son Jesus is now ours also." (LB)

St. Paul is at pains to emphasize the absolute certainty of the Christian hope. He underlines the nature of our relationship with God by describing those who are believers in Christ as, not only children of God, nor only heirs of God, but also co-heirs with Christ. He wants to make sure that no one misses his point about our future inheritance. As a teacher he does not want to take anything for granted. He restates what may seem to be obvious but which is often overlooked. He is anxious that we should understand and enjoy the meaning of what it means to be heirs of the kingdom of God.

Christ shares his inheritance with us

By describing us as co-heirs with Christ, he explains how we become heirs – not by our own merits, not by what we have done, not because God arbitrarily decided to bless us, but because of our relationship with Christ. Without Christ we would not be inheriting the kingdom at all. We inherit because Christ shares his inheritance with us.

Hebrews 1:2 reminds us that God "in these last days has spoken to us by his Son, whom he appointed heir of all things." Christ is the heir, and we only become heirs because we are incorporated into Christ, because we, by faith, are united with Christ. We become heirs because of our faith-union with Christ. We are no longer only in Adam, as natural, sinful human beings. When we put our trust in

Christ, and follow him, we became 'in Christ.' All that Christ has won by his life, death and resurrection, is given to us. All blessings come to us because of our relationship to him. Our relationship to God is through Christ. "To him who overcomes, I will give the right to sit with me on my throne, just as I overcame and sat down with my Father on his throne." (Revelation 3:21)

See the glory – the vision of God

Jesus prayed that his followers would be with him, that they might see his glory, and share his love in the future. "Father, I want those you have given me to be with me where I am, and to see my glory, the glory you have given me because you loved me before the creation of the world." (John 17:24) He looks for them to be with him so that they may see the glory that the Father has given him. What that glory means will be described later in Romans 8. William Temple attempts to explain what Jesus said.

"The perfect love of the Father for the Son and of the Son for the Father – which is the Holy Spirit – is the glory of the Godhead. It is eternal. The prayer of the Lord for his disciples is that they may see, may contemplate with adoration, that glory. His longing is that they may be with him and behold the glory which the Father eternally bestows on him is not chiefly for his sake but for theirs; for this is the Vision of God, the Beatific Vision, the infinite joy of the finite soul."[1]

[1] William Temple, *Readings in St. John's Gospel*, Macmillan, London, 1952, 330

Glory here then is perfect love which is eternal, and is revealed in the Godhead. Jesus wants us to see what that love looks like. In this life our love is partial, temporal, limited, and flawed compared with the love of God. "We see but a poor reflection as in a mirror; then we shall see face to face. Now I know in part, then I shall know fully, even as I am fully known." (1 Corinthians 13:12)

Inheritance is tied to relationship with the benefactor

Jesus has already promised us that he was going to prepare a place for us. "In my father's house are many rooms…I am going there to prepare a place for you. And if I go and prepare a place for you, I will come back and take you to be with me that you also may be where I am." (John 14:2,3) Our inheritance is secured by Christ in his Father's house. We will be with him, where he is, and see his glory.

This is why a relationship with Christ is so important for eternal life. Our future hope is tied to our relationship with Christ. The future inheritance in the kingdom is described in terms of the glory of Christ. We don't just believe in eternal life, or heaven, or a future life in the abstract, but an eternal life in Christ, a heaven in which Christ is ruling, and we with him, a future life in a place which Christ has prepared for us. That is why knowing Christ, following Christ, living with Christ, is so important in this life, to prepare us for the life to come. It is our only real hope, our only assurance of our inheritance. Inheritance is tied to relationship with the benefactor. If there is no relationship we do not qualify for inheritance. Our saving relationship with Christ guarantees our inheritance.

Our relationship with Christ is crucial

If this is so, then our relationship with Christ is crucial. We cannot diminish it in an effort to appear being impartial to adherents of other religions. Whatever their belief in the future life, ours depends upon our saving relationship with Christ. Absent of that relationship, that inheritance, we have no assurance of eternal life. Neither, we believe, can they. All the more reason why we would want to share that gift with them so that they can enjoy it.

Christ-centered or Christless?

How central is Christ to your faith? Michael Horton maintains that, in many churches the message is one of self-help, and that God exists only for our benefit. “Christless Christianity. Sounds a bit harsh doesn’t it? A little shallow, sometimes distracted, even a little human-centered rather than Christ-centered from time to time, but Christless? Let me be a little more precise about what I am assuming to be the regular diet in many churches across America today: ‘do more, try harder.’ I think this is the pervasive message across the spectrum today….I think our doctrine has been forgotten, assumed, ignored, and even misshaped and distorted by the habits and rituals of daily life in a narcissistic culture."[2]

To be a co-heir with Christ is to share in his divine inheritance. It is something that we receive by grace through faith. It is not the result of doing more and trying harder to be a better person. It is not a matter of self-improvement but of God's perfect love.

[2] Michael Horton, *Christless Christianity: The Alternative Gospel of the American Church*, Baker, Grand Rapids, 2008, p.17

10

SUFFERING ON THE ROAD TO GLORY

"...co- heirs with Christ, if indeed we share in his sufferings in order that we may also share in his glory." (Romans 8:17)

AS we honor, on Memorial Day, those who have suffered and died on our behalf in war, we remember that the inheritance of Christ includes, not only glory, but also suffering: "we share in his sufferings in order that we may also share in his glory." (Romans 8:17) Before we enter into our inheritance we have to pass through suffering as Christ himself did on our behalf. On the road to Emmaus, Jesus had to remind the disciples, who were discouraged because of the Cross, that the prophets had spoken of the sufferings of the Messiah. "Did not the Christ have to suffer these things and then enter his glory. And beginning with Moses and all the Prophets, he explained to them what was said in the Scriptures concerning himself." (Luke 24:26,27) The story told by the Scriptures is of the Creation and Fall, the terribleness of sin and judgment, and the greatness of God's love and mercy. The people of God had to learn obedience by the things they suffered, and Jesus showed his humanity by doing the same (Hebrews 5:8). Like Jesus, we are called to take up our cross and follow him (Luke 9:23, 14:27).

Sharing in the sufferings of Christ

Our sufferings in this life, are to be seen as participation in the sufferings of Christ, indeed the suffering of God for his creation. Just as it was necessary for Christ to have to suffer before he entered his glory, so we have to suffer before we enter into our inheritance in Christ. "I want to know Christ and the power of his resurrection and the fellowship of sharing in his sufferings, becoming like him in his death, and so, somehow, to attain to the resurrection from the dead." (Philippians 3:10,11)

God's way of creation and salvation is the way of the cross, the way of suffering. The divine DNA of the universe is that of suffering. Nothing worthwhile is accomplished without suffering. To attempt to avoid suffering is futile. To present Christianity in terms other than that of the Cross is to present a false Gospel. To expect that life will always go smoothly is unrealistic. To believe that the mark of God's blessing in your life is the absence of suffering is to repeat the error of Job's comforters. To think that we can always be happy in this life is delusional. To deny the reality of evil and the biblical diagnosis that we are all sinners under judgment is to live in a fantasy world. To make the central goal in your life to feel good about yourself is egotistical.

Unfortunately this is the operating philosophy of many churches today.

Marsha Witten in her study, *"All is Forgiven: The Secular Message in American Protestantism*", recounts an afternoon on Good Friday. While she was listening to Bach's, *St. Matthew Passion*, "with antiphonal choirs calling out sorrowfully to Jesus in his grave," the daily mail arrived and she opened the thickest envelope first. It was promotional material for a new church launching in her area:

> *Hi Neighbor!*
>
> *At last! a new church for those who have given up on church services! Let's face it. Many people aren't active in church these days.*
>
> *WHY?*
>
> *Too often*
>
> - *the sermons are boring and don't relate to daily living*
> - *many churches seem more interested in your wallet than in you*
> - *members are unfriendly to visitors*
> - *you wonder about the quality of the nursery care for your little ones*
>
> *Do you think attending church should be enjoyable?*
>
> *WELL, WE'VE GOT GOOD NEWS FOR YOU!*
>
> *Valley Church is a new church designed to meet your needs. At Valley Church you*
>
> - *meet new friends and get to know your neighbors*

- *enjoy exciting music with a contemporary flavor*
- *hear positive, practical messages which uplift you each week*
  How to feel good about yourself
  How to overcome depression
  How to have a full and successful life
  Learning to handle your money without it handling you
  The secrets of successful family living
  How to overcome stress
- *Trust your children to the care of dedicated nursery workers*

WHY NOT GET A LIFT
INSTEAD OF A LETDOWN THIS SUNDAY?[1]

This is the contemporary marketing of the Gospel. It is consumer oriented using secular marketing techniques. Its message is: *God loves us and wants to make us feel good. Life is meant to be fun all the time.*

"Everything is okay – without any mention of Christ's self-sacrifice as the only way of reconciliation. Since, as a rule, God's love apparently overwhelms his justice and holiness, the 'good news' offered here eliminates any need for the actual story recorded in the Gospels. If God's love so easily ignores his justice, holiness, and righteousness, then Christ's death upon the cross seems like a cruel waste. Witten writes, 'It is "negative feelings," not an

---

[1] Quoted by Michael Horton, op,cit., p.49

objectively negative danger, that these sermons stress as being solved by the gospel.'"[2]

Suffering cannot be avoided in life. Christ had to suffer and die. When he explained to the disciples "that he must go to Jerusalem and suffer many things at the hands of the elders, chief priests and teachers of the law, and that he must be killed and on the third day be raised to life, Peter took him aside and began to rebuke him, 'Never, Lord! This shall never happen to you!' Jesus turned and said to Peter, 'Get behind me Satan! You are a stumbling block to me; you do not have in mind the things of God but the things of men.' (Matthew 16:21-23) Jesus then told the other disciples that anyone who came after him must take up his cross – i.e.suffer.

Preachers who fail to see suffering as the path to glory, and do not honor the cross, and do not see suffering as the school for learning obedience and ultimately redemptive, are, like Peter, at that point in his life, immature. They have in mind the things of men, not the things of God.

How suffering can be endured

Suffering is the path to glory. Suffering can only be endured if:

1. it has a purpose,
2. if it leads to something worthwhile, and
3. if we can be assured that it will one day end.

The rest of Romans 8 assures us that suffering has a purpose, it will be worthwhile, and it will end. St. Peter in

---

[2] Michael Horton, op.cit., p.56

his maturity reminds us: "Dear friends, do not be surprised at the painful trial you are suffering, as though something strange were happening to you. But rejoice, that you participate in the sufferings of Christ, so that you may be overjoyed when his glory is revealed." (1 Peter 4:12,13)

Redemption of suffering

"There is much to be said about the Christian meaning of suffering.....Perhaps our suffering is deeply connected with the possibility of salvation for human beings; perhaps we share in Christ's suffering in a way that our suffering too is salvific, and perhaps even essential to the plan of salvation. Someone who suffers may then look forward to receiving the divine gratitude for taking part in this project of salvation, and to enjoying forever the love and approval of God; she may well concur with Paul: 'We are fellow heirs with Christ, provided we suffer with him in order that we may also be glorified with him.' She may thus reflect that human suffering is in a way an occasion for gratitude. There is another way in which it is perhaps an occasion of gratitude. It is plausible to think that the best possible worlds God could have actualized contain the unthinkable great good of divine incarnation and redemption – but then, of course, also sin and suffering. God chooses one of these worlds to be actual – and in it, humankind suffers. Still, in this world there is also the marvelous opportunity for redemption and for eternal fellowship with

God, an inconceivably great good that vastly outweighs the suffering we are called upon to endure."[3]

William Stuntz, renowned professor at Harvard Law School, died of cancer at age of 52. He lived with severe and constant pain for over ten years, an agony he likened to having a blaring alarm clock strapped to his ear with no power to lower the volume. He testified to the divine redemption of suffering, that God works through the curses of our lives to bring about blessing. "I may never know precisely what form that redemption takes, and that's fine with me. It's enough to know that I do not, and we do not, suffer pointlessly. Our God delights in taking the worst things in life and using them to produce the best things in life."[4]

G.A. Studdert–Kennedy was a chaplain in the first World War. He wrote many memorable poems, but one, *The Suffering God*, captured the heart of the Gospel. Here are some lines from it.

Father, if He, the Christ, were Thy Revealer,
Truly the First Begotten of the Lord,
Then must Thou be a Suff'rer and a Healer,
Pierced to the heart by the sorrow of the
sword.

Then must it mean, not only that Thy sorrow
Smote Thee that once upon the lonely tree,
But that to-day, to-night, and on the morrow,
Still it will come, O Gallant God, to thee.

---

[3] Alvin Plantinga, *Warranted Christian Belief*, Oxford University Press, 2000, 488,489

[4] Timothy Dalrymple, Patheos blog, March 22, 2011

Give me for light, the sunshine of Thy sorrow,
    Give me for shelter shadow of Thy Cross,
Give me to share the glory of Thy morrow,
    Gone from my heart the bitterness of Loss.

11

THE HOPE OF GLORY

"I consider that our present sufferings are not worth comparing with the glory that will be revealed in us." (Romans 8:18)

What is glory? The dictionary definitions are "great honor and admiration won by doing something important or valuable; fame, renown; the condition of highest achievement, prosperity; radiant beauty or splendor, magnificence; heaven and its bliss; our best, our happiest."

In the Bible it describes a state, a condition of life that reflects the presence of a pure and holy God. In Isaiah's vision in the temple, when he saw the Lord seated on a throne, he heard the angels calling to one another: "Holy, holy, holy is the Lord Almighty; the whole earth is full of his glory." (Isaiah 6:3) This is the indescribable splendor of God, beautiful, overflowing with goodness, power, and purity.

Glory is presented in the New Testament as the hope of the Christian believer. Jesus prayed to the Father that we might see his glory: "the glory you have given me because you loved me before the creation of the world." (John 17:24) Just as Jesus had to suffer before he was glorified, so also must we. As St. Paul puts it, "We share in his sufferings in order that we may also share in his glory." (Roman 8:17) But the presence of Christ within us enables us to anticipate the future with real hope. The message of the gospel gives us hope for the glory that is to come. "The glorious riches of this mystery, which is Christ in you, the hope of glory." (Colossians 1:27)

Christ indwelling us enables us to achieve our best and highest purpose and fulfillment. As we seek to magnify the presence of Christ in our lives we increase the glory. So we sing and pray:

Let the beauty of Jesus be seen in me,
All his wonderful passion and purity.[1]

We need spiritual cataract surgery

The word 'glory' carries with it associations of visible light and splendor – moral brilliance – as in the Transfiguration ("His face shone like the sun, and his clothes became as white as the light." Matt.17:2), and on the Damascus Road ("I saw a light from heaven, brighter than the sun, blazing around me" Acts 26:13). The radiance was recognized as a symbol for spiritual glory – the thin place between heaven and earth denoting the presence of God. We

---

[1] Rev. Tom Jones, *The Broadman Hymnal*, 1940, Nashville

need spiritual cataract surgery in order to see the earth filled with glory, and the hope in heaven that it anticipates.

St. Paul writes, "I pray also that the eyes of your heart may be enlightened in order that you may know the hope to which he has called you, the riches of his glorious inheritance in the saints." (Ephesians 1:18 NIV) "That you may receive that inner illumination of the spirit which will make you realize how great is the hope to which he is calling you – the magnificence and splendor of the inheritance promised to Christians." (JBP)

Humanity was originally designed to live in the presence of God. But "all have sinned and fall short of the glory of God." (Romans 3:23) Without God, we are bound to fall short of his glory; but in Christ it is attained; and to be engaged in fulfilling such a destiny by suffering 'in Christ' is a glorious thing (Eph.3:13, cf. Rom.8:18,21). The wealth of glory found in Christ is the ground for the Christian's confidence in a glorious destiny to come.

The key to the understanding of the whole of human history

"We were never meant to 'come short of the glory of God,' but it has happened to us as the result of sin. Such is the truth about all of us born into this world. Man is not what he is meant to be. This is basic biblical teaching. Man has lost the glory that he originally possessed, and tends to demonstrate his loss in every aspect of his behavior. This is the essential tragedy of man; this is the real problem of mankind. It is the only way of understanding the world as it is today. Man still has a kind of memory and recollection of what he once was, and he is always trying to return to it and to persuade himself that he is succeeding. But failure dogs his steps. Hence his frustration. Now that is the key to the understanding of the whole of human history, the explanation of all the intense effort which man puts forth as he seeks the glory which he feels belongs to him. But he can never get it, he cannot find it. Here we find the explanation of man's restlessness and unhappiness...

Man is meant for glory

What causes this restlessness? The fact is that no one is satisfied with what he has. The world is full of ambition, rivalry, jealousy and pride. Why? It is just this matter of trying to be what we feel deep within us we were meant to be, and ought to be....Because man lacks understanding of this truth he is always bringing forward schemes, always making his proposals, always confident and assured, always believing that he is about to arrive. Suddenly, everything crashes again; and he is back where he was before, or even further back. The history of mankind illustrates this principle of cycles. There is no steady advance; for a while we seem to be progressing well; then suddenly we begin to experience set-backs. Events, we find, proceed in cycles, civilizations rise and fall after the same manner. But, rise or fall, man retains the feeling that he is meant for glory."[2]

---

[2] D. Martyn Lloyd-Jones, *Romans, The Final Perseverance of the Saints*, Zondervan, Grand Rapids, 1976, pp.4-6

Suffering is temporary, glory is eternal

We *are* meant for glory! Just as, in this life, we share in Christ's sufferings, in the life to come we will surely share in his glory. This is the Christian hope. That is why we can endure the sufferings of this life. St. Paul puts them in perspective with what is to come. "I consider that our present sufferings are not worth comparing with the glory that will be revealed in us." (Romans 8:18) Our sufferings are temporary, while our glory is eternal.

"Therefore, we do not lose heart. Though outwardly we are wasting away, yet inwardly we are being renewed day by day. For our light and momentary troubles are achieving for us an eternal glory that far outweighs them all. So we fix our eyes not on what is seen, but on what is unseen. For what is seen is temporary, but what is unseen is eternal." (2 Corinthians 4:16-18) Our focus is to be on the future hope of glory, not on the sufferings of this present life.

We do not lose heart

"Therefore, we do not lose heart." This speaks to our condition. What makes us 'lose heart?' What discourages us, depresses us? We get preoccupied with our present difficulties, our present sufferings, our present challenges, our present anxieties and fears. We fall short of God's glory. We feel defeated. We don't have the get up and go we used to have. Life is more difficult than it used to be. The old remedies don't work. We lose heart. What is God's solution for us? Look forward to the glory that is in store for you in

Christ. Keep your eyes upon heaven. Stay in the Word each day. Let the Scriptures educate your perspective and fill your mind. Pray at all times for the protection and guidance of the Spirit.

"So we're not giving up. How could we? Even though on the outside it often looks like things are falling apart on us, on the inside, where God is making new life, not a day goes by without his unfolding grace. These hard times are small potatoes compared to the coming good times, the lavish celebration prepared for us. There's far more here than meets the eye. The things we see now are here today, gone tomorrow. But the things we can't see now will last forever." (2 Corinthians 4:16-18 *The Message*)

Helen Keller, although deaf and blind in this life, looked forward to the hope of glory in the life to come. "For three things I thank God every day of my life: thanks that he has vouchsafed me knowledge of his works; deep thanks that he has set in my darkness the lamp of faith; deep, deepest thanks that I have another life to look forward to – a life joyous with light and flowers and heavenly song."

C.S Lewis, in *The Great Divorce*, attempts to describe the entry procession of an unknown lady into heaven. She was preceded by bright Spirits and youthful shapes and musicians, also gigantic people like emeralds dancing and throwing flowers before her. She was surrounded by young men and women, cats, dogs, birds and horses. "Every beast and bird that came near her had its place in her love. In her they became themselves. And now the abundance of life she has in Christ from the Father flows over into them....It is like when you throw a stone into a pool, and the concentric waves spread out further and further. Who knows where it will end? Redeemed humanity is still young, it has hardly come to its full strength. But already there is joy enough in the little finger of a great saint such as yonder lady to waken all the dead things of the universe into life... The Bright Spirits came forward to receive her, singing as they came:

> *The Happy Trinity is her home: nothing can trouble her joy.*
>
> *She is the bird that evades every net: the wild deer that leaps every pitfall.*
>
> *Like the mother bird to its chickens or a shield to the arm'd knight: so is the Lord to her mind, in his unchanging lucidity.*
>
> *Bogies will not scare her in the dark: bullets will not frighten her in the day......*
>
> *He details immortal gods to attend her: upon every road where she must travel.*
>
> *They take her hand at hard places: she will not stub her toes in the dark.*
>
> *She may walk among Lions and rattlesnakes: among dinosaurs and nurseries of lionets.*
>
> *He fills her brim full with immensity of life: he leads her to see the world's desire."*[3]

You are meant for glory. Do not fall short of it. When you make room for Christ in your life, make him your priority, and seek first his will, you will find that you enjoy the hope of glory.

---

[3] C.S. Lewis, *The Great Divorce*, Macmillan, New York, 1968, pp.106-120

12

THE REVELATION OF GLORY

"I consider that our present sufferings are not worth comparing with the glory that will be revealed in us. The creation waits in eager expectation for the sons of God to be revealed." (Romans 8:18,19)

"This paragraph, from verse 18 to verse 25, is the classic statement on the question of suffering. It is not the only one, of course, but in many ways it is the most profound statement of the suffering of the Christian in this present life."[1] So wrote Dr. Martyn Lloyd-Jones, of Westminster Chapel, London.

It tells us that we should look at suffering in terms of purpose, its end, its healing, its redemption. Philosophers would call it a teleological perspective: Greek, *telos* = end; the doctrine of final causes, the view that developments are due to the purpose or design that is served by them, e.g. a *tele*scope brings the object in view, the end in view, it gives you a closer perspective on what is far away. The Bible

---

[1] D. Martyn Lloyd-Jones, op.cit., p14

continually exhorts us to look ahead to the goal of our existence in order to make sense of this present life. This is the difference between the scientific method and the Biblical message. Science looks at the past for evidence, and the Bible looks to the future. "Evolutionary theory may offer an account of what has been observed and is being observed, but it cannot predict future specifics."[2] The New Testament sees the future as providing meaning and purpose for the present. Jesus and the apostles talk about the rewards at the last day awarded to those who are faithful. St. Paul is saying that our present sufferings, as difficult as they are, can be borne by us if we know what lies ahead of us.

Future rewards for suffering

Jesus is the great example of this attitude. "Let us fix our eyes on Jesus, the author and perfecter of faith, who for the joy set before him endured the cross, scorning its shame, and sat down at the right hand of the throne of God." (Hebrews 12:2) The sufferings of the cross were insignificant compared to the joy set before him. His reward was the exaltation of humanity to the right hand of God. We are likewise encouraged to look beyond our present difficulties to God's promised rewards.

What is our reward for all the suffering of this present life? What is it that can possibly help us to endure the troubles that we have to go through? What will make all the pain worthwhile?

---

[2] Alister McGrath, *A Fine-Tuned Universe*, p.194

To be able to handle suffering in this world we have to have a view of the world to come. Without an eternal perspective, without a teleological perspective, you cannot make sense of the sufferings of this life. Without a belief in an eternal reward, you cannot enjoy hope. We must have knowledge of the joy that is set before us if we are going to be able to bear our cross in this life.

Future joy

We would not undergo surgery or treatment of any kind unless we thought it would result in a better condition, that it would help us to live more fully. I have just had cataract surgery, and it has been worth it. I am about to have some teeth crowned for the second time. I hope it will be worth it! It costs a small fortune these days. We could not face our daily lives with all the challenges we encounter if we did not think that it would result in some future joy.

What is that joy that is set before us? It is when the sons of God are revealed. Today we are flesh and blood, sinners, falling short of the glory of God. We say things we shouldn't. We do things we shouldn't. We don't say or do things we should. We are damaged goods. The sins of the fathers are continued in us. We are part of a polluted and fallen world. We are not beautiful, pure and good. There is no part of us that is perfect. But one day, we have been promised that we will be cleaned up, healed, made whole, and we shall be saved. We will have all the vigor of youth and all the wisdom of age. We will look as though we are brimming with health and beauty, while exhibiting the virtues of spiritual maturity. We will be in the twenties physically, with sixties emotional intelligence. Instead of seeing ourselves as we are now in the mirror we will be looking at ourselves as we remember we were.

There will be no more "death, or mourning, or crying or pain, for the old order of things will be passed away." (Revelation 21:4) Everything will be made new. What we shall be will be revealed to all the creation. In fact, the universe, "waits in eager expectation" for this to occur. This suggests the "stretching of the neck, craning forward to see something which is approaching, of the whole splendid theatre of the universe and of all the manifold sub-human life within it as eagerly awaiting the revelation of the sons of God."[3] We will be making our debut on the stage of the universe.

Incognito

We are sons and daughters of God now, but our final destiny is not yet revealed. We are in disguise. There is still much to be done to spiritually develop us into what we are meant to become. We are still a work in progress. Again, Jesus is an example of what Paul means by this.

Jesus lived on this earth as God the Son. He was born in a natural way, in poor circumstances. He was raised as a carpenter's son in a regular family with brothers. He took over his father's trade, and was known as a carpenter. His glory was hidden, it was veiled. His contemporaries saw him as a prophet, and a teacher. He was also a healer, and a miracle-worker. He was God come in disguise, incognito, so that no one would know him by direct knowledge but would have to exercise faith.

---

[3] Charles Cranfield, *Romans*, Eerdmans, Grand Rapids, 1985, p.195

Many saw him as a troublemaker, a critic of the religious authorities, an iconoclast, who made life difficult for the national leaders of his day. They thought him blasphemous and irreverent rather than holy and exemplary. Some accused him of being demonic, an agent of Satan rather than the voice of God. Yet, to those who believed in him, and who were open to his revelation, he was the Son of God. One day he will be revealed from heaven in glory and honor. All the world will acknowledge him as Lord of All. "At that time men will see the Son of Man coming in clouds with great power and glory." (Mark 13:26)

Future revelation

Just as Jesus will one day be revealed for who he really is, and all creation shall acknowledge directly his power and great glory, so too we will be revealed for who we will become. This knowledge will sustain us in the midst of life with all its problems and difficulties. The perishable will be clothed with the imperishable, and the mortal with immortality.

"How great is the love the Father has lavished on us, that we should be called children of God! And that is what we are! The reason the world does not know us is that it did not know him. Dear friends, now we are children of God and what we will be has not yet been made known. But we know that when he appears, we shall be like him, for we shall see him as he is. Everyone who has this hope in him purifies himself, just as he is pure." (1 John 3:1-3)

If now we have a glimpse of what it means to be the child of God in our relationship with a loving heavenly Father, when Christ appears in glory there will be yet more overwhelming experiences for us. He will appear, and we shall appear just like him. We shall see him as he really is, without the humble disguise of his servanthood. He will no longer be incognito but revealed as Lord of all. Because of this hope we will be able to gradually become like him. The glory will be revealed in us.

If we know that this joy is set before us, we gain the strength to persevere in the midst of things we cannot understand. We run the race, we keep the faith, because at the finish line there is a crown of righteousness to be awarded to us. (2 Timothy 4:8) This glory is revealed to all creation. We are surrounded by a great cloud of witnesses as we run with perseverance the race marked out for us. (Hebrews 12:1)

The humble will be exalted

Knowledge of this revelation will also cause us to value those who in this world appear to be insignificant and of no account. The lowest of the low, the handicapped, the mentally challenged, the poor, the weak and the disadvantaged, those who have suffered much in this life, may, one day, have the glory revealed in them. As the creation waits in eager expectation for the sons and daughters of God to be revealed we may be in for a surprise. Those who have rejected the Lord, who have been indifferent to his call, who have been deaf to his voice, and blind to his presence, will exclude themselves from his glory. The great and the mighty, the healthy and the beautiful, the rich and the famous, the successful and the popular, may be relegated to the rear, and it is a little child who will lead them. (Isaiah 11:6) For you must become as a little child to enter the kingdom of heaven.

"Then will the eyes of the blind be opened and the ears of the deaf unstopped. Then will the lame leap like a deer and the mute tongue will shout for joy." (Isaiah 35:5,6) "Those who are wise will shine like the brightness of the heavens, and those who lead many to righteousness, like the stars for ever and ever." (Daniel 12:3)

What about you? Do you want to make sense of the sufferings of this life? Do you want to enter into the joy that is set before you? Do you want to enter into the revelation of the glory that Jesus has prepared for you? Then commit yourself to fix your eyes on Jesus every day and follow him in faith, by looking forward to the goal of heaven.

13

THE LIBERATION OF CREATION

"For the creation was subjected to frustration, not by its own choice, but by the will of the one who subjected it, in hope that the creation itself will be liberated from its bondage to decay and brought into the glorious freedom of the children of God." (Romans 8:20,21)

Some of the most fundamental questions of human existence are "How do we make sense of the world around us? What is going on in the universe?" The teaching of the Bible and the perspective of Christian faith provides a map of reality that enables us to discover clues to the meaning of the universe. Alister McGrath comments on the words of C.S. Lewis: 'I believe in Christianity as I believe the Sun has risen, not only because I see it, but because by it I see everything else.'

"For Lewis, the Christian faith was like an intellectual sun, illuminating and irradiating the rich conceptual landscape of the natural world, enabling the observer to make sense of, and hence appreciate, the intricate tapestry of human experience and thought. Cultivating the art of seeing is the key to unlocking the meaning of the world."[1]

In Romans 8, St. Paul is helping us 'make sense of, and hence appreciate, the intricate tapestry of human experience and thought.' He provides a map of reality that enables us to discover clues to the meaning of the universe. This map reveals a process of salvation and restoration of the whole creation. He uses the analogy of human aging to help us see the whole creation as a system that is aging, to enable us to make sense of the world around us, as well as our own lives.

The Effects of Human Rebellion

The story of the Fall of Adam and Eve in Genesis 3 includes, not only the Fall of Man and Woman from God's presence, through their desire to be like God, but also its effects upon the rest of creation. "Cursed is the ground because of you; through painful toil you will eat of it all the days of your life. It will produce thorns and thistles for you, and you will eat the plants of the field." (Genesis 3:17,18) This curse will not be lifted until the new heavens and the new earth portrayed in Revelation – "No longer will there be any curse." (3:22) Humanity, when opposing the will of God, degrades the natural world. Nature today is at peril owing to over-consumption. The planet, in many parts, is plundered and poisoned by the selfishness of man. Our hubris, our desire to play God, threatens the devastation of creation.

---

[1] Alister E. McGrath, *A Fine-Tuned Universe*, Westminster John Knox, Louisville, 2009, 21

St. Paul sums up the result of God's curse by the one word, *frustration*. It means 'emptiness, futility, purposelessness, transitoriness'.[2] "Once humans seek to discover the full possibilities of their selfhood through disobedient self-assertion rather than through drawing closer to the will of God who made them, their relationship with each other and with their surroundings is at once distorted. Mutual trust is replaced by blame, envy and violence; what has been received as gift has to be worked for, struggled for."[3] The creation, viewed as an evolutionary process, is futile, with the extinction of over 98 per cent of the species that have ever lived.

Entropy - Reversed

The creation is in 'bondage to decay.' The second law of thermodynamics speaks about entropy – the inevitable and steady deterioration of a system or society. The universe is aging, and in the process is deteriorating, declining, decomposing, and dying. God has subjected the universe to this bondage to decay to remind us of our dependency, our mortality, and our sinfulness. Sin is also ecological. We are meant to be stewards of creation. The creation as a whole, not just humanity, is in need of redemption.

But Paul reminds us that the creation is subjected by God to frustration and decay as a prelude to the hope of liberation. "The story of creation is a forward-looking story in which a tragic state is being transformed, with much

---

[2] William F. Arndt and F. Wilbur Gingrich, *Greek-English Lexicon of the New Testament.*

[3] Christopher Southgate, *The Groaning of Creation*, Westminster John Knox, Louisville, 2008, 28

suffering and struggle, into one of liberation."[4] This liberation will parallel the glorious freedom of the children of God. What God is doing for his children, he will do also for the rest of creation. There will be a new creation, a new heaven and a new earth. Decay, one day, will be reversed. New life will be produced. This is the hope of the Bible, the good news of Jesus.

"The desert and the parched land will be glad; the wilderness will rejoice and blossom. Like the crocus, it will burst into bloom; it will rejoice greatly and shout for joy." (Isaiah 35:1,2) Jesus talked about 'the renewal of all things." (Matthew 19:28) Peter spoke about the 'restoration of all things." (Acts 3:21)

"The general promise of the renovation and transformation of nature is plain, including the eradication of all harmful elements and their replacement by righteousness, peace, harmony, joy and security."[5]

No more let sins and sorrows grow,
Nor thorns infest the ground;
He comes to make His blessings flow
Far as the curse is found,
Far as the curse is found.[6]

This age in which we live is revealed as a temporal boot camp which is meant to prepare us for the day of liberation which is at hand. In this temporal boot camp there is frustration, and bondage to decay, but we can endure it, because we have the hope of graduation - liberation into the

---

[4] Southgate, op. cit., 94
[5] Stott, op. cit., 240
[6] Isaac Watts, *Joy to the World*

glorious freedom of the children of God. Boot camp is essential, because in it we learn the skills, and acquire the knowledge which will enable us to survive and fulfill our mission. This life separates out the 'men from the boys'- those who can follow orders, and save lives, from those who can't. It separates out those who can look out for their comrades, and those who would abandon them for self-interest. It separates out those who are willing to give their lives for something greater than themselves, and those who won't.

Making sense of our lives

How does this map of reality help us to make sense of our lives and the world around us? It enables us to understand our own frustrations, our feeling sometimes that what we do has no purpose or meaning. It enables us to understand the frustrations of the rest of humanity in its search for solutions to its problems. Generation after generation seeks to deal with its frustrations by various methods: spiritual, psychological, financial, social, political and military. This frustration is the result of the Fall. It is part of the sinful human condition, as is our bondage to decay – our deterioration. But Jesus comes to give us hope, that we and the whole creation will be, one day, liberated from this bondage to decay, and brought into glorious freedom. It is this hope that sustains us with clues to the meaning of the universe. His resurrection overcame death and decay, and ushered in the new age into which we are born: "an inheritance that can never perish, spoil or fade." (1 Peter 1:4)

"The book of Revelation portrays every creature in heaven and on earth and under the earth and in the sea joining the saints who surround the throne of God to sing God's praises (Revelation 5:9-14). If such redemption comes, it will be God's doing. In a world where what lies behind us has actually managed to happen, almost anything can happen....The same God that lured protozoans into persons may still work on scales that we cannot imagine scientifically....The miracle of a new heaven and a new earth would be a lesser miracle than the fact that this past and present heaven and earth are and have been here in the first place. The story of the last several billion years has not been so much the loss of value as of its transformation into new levels of attainment and power."[7]

The good news is that Jesus has given us this hope of liberation and glorious freedom.

---

[7] Holmes Rolston, III, *Does Nature Need To Be Redeemed?*, Zygon: Journal of Religion and Science 29 (no.2 1994:228)

14

THE SUFFERING OF CREATION

"We know that the whole creation has been groaning as in the pains of childbirth right up to the present time." (Romans 8:22)

One of the most difficult challenges to faith is to be found in the suffering of the world. Skeptics ask, "How can a good God permit such terrible suffering? If he is good and powerful he would prevent it. If he doesn't prevent such suffering he is either not good, or not powerful, or he does not exist."

We not only see suffering around the world, we see it in our own relationships. All of us have experienced suffering in our families, our children, disappointed hopes, our marriages, our finances, our own physical and mental health. How does our faith in a good and powerful God help us in our sufferings?

It does not help to deny the reality and pervasiveness of suffering. Some Christians view the world through rose-colored spectacles. They see the hand of God in the beautiful design of the world, but overlook the essential nature of suffering as part of creation. Suffering is built into the creation. It is through suffering that life comes forth. It is through suffering that life is nourished. It is through suffering that reproduction and survival occurs.

St. Paul was clear-eyed when he wrote, "We know that the whole creation has been groaning as in the pains of childbirth right up to the present time." (Romans 8:22)

Design and Suffering

Arguments for the existence of God often use the argument from design. Believers may claim that they see the hand of God in the beauty of nature. Yet the design of the universe also includes billions of years of suffering. An atheist will see the violence and cruelty of predators in the food pyramid, and the Darwinian theory of the survival of the fittest, as evidence of no design, no purpose, no evil or good, nothing but a blind, pitiless indifference in the universe. But while the distinguished American environmental philosopher and theologian Holmes Ralston III also sees the creation as full of suffering, it is also "orderly, prolific, efficient, selecting for adaptive fit, exuberant, complex, diverse, regenerating life generation after generation."[1]

It is important to see the creation as it is, as a whole, and not through overly romantic spectacles. All creation

---

[1] quoted in Southgate, op. cit., 3

suffers. Animals struggle with chronic disease, or the effects of parasites, or die lingering deaths from inefficient predator attacks, or their own injuries. Suffering is endemic and intrinsic to the development of creation. It does not help for Christians to turn a blind eye to suffering, to ignore it. Our faith has to accept suffering as part of life, just as Jesus accepted suffering and death on the Cross for us.

Realism in the Artist

This realistic view of life should inform the artist. John Ruskin in *Modern Painters* (1860) reflects upon a landscape in the Scottish Highlands. "Ruskin insists that God does not wish us to see only the 'bright side' of nature. God has given us 'two sides' of nature and intends us to see them both. Those who see nature only in positive terms are failing to see it as it actually is. To make his point Ruskin points to an unnamed 'zealous' Scottish clergyman who was determined to see the landscape as a witness to the 'goodness of God.' And so he described it in terms of 'nothing but sunshine, and fresh breezes, and bleating lambs, and clean tartans, and all kinds of pleasantness.'

Yet Ruskin dismisses this as inept. The zealous clergyman has chosen to see what he wishes to see, not to see what is actually there. For Ruskin, 'to see clearly' lies at the heart of poetry, prophecy, and religion. How can one live with such a blatant failure to see clearly? How can nature be sunlit without there being shadows? Ruskin offers an alternative viewing of a Highland landscape, stressing its moral and aesthetic ambivalence:

> It is a little valley of soft turf, enclosed in its narrow oval by jutting rocks and broad flakes of nodding fern. From one side of it to the other winds, serpentine, a clear brown stream, dropping into quicker ripple as it reaches the end of the oval field, and then, first islanding a purple and white rock with an amber pool, it dashes away into a narrow fall of foam under a thicket of mountain-ash and alder. The autumn sun, low but clear, shines on the scarlet ash-berries and on the golden birch-leaves, which, fallen here and there, when the breeze has not aught them, rest quiet in the crannies of the purple rock.

Up to this point, Ruskin echoes the somewhat one-sided sentiments of the Scottish parson. Yet the shadows, he insists, must be seen. Ruskin's mood alters as he describes the less-attractive aspects of the scene:

> Beside the rock, in the hollow under the thicket, the carcass of a ewe, drowned in the last flood, lies nearly bare to the bone, its white ribs protruding through the skin, raven-torn; and the rags of its wool still flickering from the branches that first stayed it as the stream swept it down…At the turn of the brook, I see a man fishing, with a boy and a dog – a picturesque and pretty group enough certainly, if they had not been there all day starving. I know them, and I know the dog's ribs also, which are nearly as bare as the dead ewe's; and the child's wasted shoulders,

> cutting his old tartan jacket through, so sharp
> are they.

Ruskin's point cannot be challenged, and there is nothing to be gained by gilding his lily through further comment. There is a shadowy side to nature, which cannot be denied or softened by even the most romantic imagination."[2]

The suffering of God in creation

Yet the scriptures teach us that creation is good. "Good" means appropriate to the purpose of which it was created. Creation gives rise to great values of beauty, diversity and ingenuity. It is good because it is the Lord's – "The earth is the Lord's and everything in it, the world, and all who live in it." (Psalm 24:1) It would seem that suffering is the only way God could give rise to the sort of world with all the values that the creation contains. Therefore the God who creates must suffer with his creation. He is in childbirth with us. Christopher Southgate writes, "I take the Cross of Christ to be the epitome of divine compassion, the moment of God's taking ultimate responsibility for the pain of creation, and – with the Resurrection – to inaugurate the transformation of creation."[3]

How can a good God permit such terrible suffering? Because "the sort of universe we have is the only sort of universe that could give rise to the range, beauty, complexity and diversity of creatures the Earth has produced."[4] Christ

---

[2] McGrath, op. cit., 81,82
[3] Op. cit., 16
[4] Southgate, op. cit., 29

created a world ("through him all things were made; without him nothing was made that has been made" - John 1:3), that "has been groaning as in the pains of childbirth right up to the present time." Christ is still in the process of creating the universe. Christ suffers in the suffering of all creation.

Life as a real Passion Play

"Rolston says, 'The secret of life is that it is a *passion play*.'...at the Passion of Christ, the good does not have its meaning without the suffering intrinsic to it."[5] Christ is in all events, with the sufferers, in a way that brings forth new life – childbirth. God is the midwife of creation. Christ suffered death for the transformation of the world. God in Christ bore the pain of the creation and human sin. We are called to participate with God in the divine transformation of the creation.

The pain and hope of childbirth

The goodness and beauty of the creation is often hidden and obscured by suffering, yet in the pain there is the hope of new life, a new birth, a new opportunity. Jesus said, "I tell you the truth, you will weep and mourn...You will grieve, but your grief will turn to joy. A woman giving birth to a child has pain because her time is come; but when her baby is born she forgets the anguish because of her joy that a child is born into the world. So with you: Now is your time of grief, but I will see you again and you will rejoice, and no one will take away your joy." (John 16:20-22)

[5] Southgate, op. cit., 46

You can see your suffering as participating in the birth of new life. "The capacity to suffer through to joy is the supreme essence of Christianity." (Holmes Rolston, III)

"Life is not beautiful all the time. But through the ugliness and pain...and loneliness there is available to every human being the fragrance of the very Presence of Christ." (Eugenia Price)

Seek His Presence, His Joy!

15

WAITING EAGERLY AND PATIENTLY

"We ourselves, who have the firstfruits of the Spirit, groan inwardly as we wait eagerly for our adoption as sons, the redemption of our bodies. But hope that is seen is no hope at all. Who hopes for what he already has? But if we hope for what we do not yet have, we wait for it patiently." (Romans 8:23-25)

How good are you at waiting? This period in our lives is a time of waiting. It is an interim period between entering into the kingdom of God by faith, and experiencing the grace of God now, and the future fulfillment of the promises of salvation in glory. "This is our Christian dilemma. Caught in the tension between what God has inaugurated (by giving us his Spirit) and what he will consummate (in our final adoption and redemption), we groan with discomfort and longing. The indwelling Spirit gives us joy, and the coming glory gives us hope, but the interim suspense gives us pain."[1]

---

[1] Stott, op. cit., 242

The anxiety of waiting

It is like waiting in the airport for your flight. You have packed and traveled to the airport. You have checked your bags and printed out your boarding pass. You have gone through security, with all its indignities! Now you are waiting to board. You are looking forward to arriving at your destination, and beginning your vacation or seeing your family; but before you can enter into that enjoyment you must endure the flight. You look across the waiting area and see a very large man or woman spread out over two seats, and pray that he or she is not going to be sitting next to you. You see the mother with the toddler that is tired and restless, and wonder whether she is going to be sitting near you. A middle-aged lady is carrying a bag from which you see the head of small dog protruding. Will you be sitting next to a dog? You groan inwardly as you contemplate having to find a space for your carry-on bag in the bin overhead. Your legs are aching, and you hope your sciatica, or arthritis, does not flair up on the flight. You watch the television and hear the newscaster announce the story of the pilot who has collapsed and died while flying, and the plane being taken over by the co-pilot. Your anxiety level rises as you contemplate the plane crashing, and wonder what the weather is going to be like on your flight. You long to be on the ground at your destination but you have to wait, and endure, and anticipate the next few hours before you can enjoy the pleasure of arriving.

You are waiting in the prep room before surgery. You are eager to get it over and done with, but you must wait patiently for your turn in the operating room. You are making the transition between independent living and assisted living. You know that you can no longer live on your own, but you hate to give up your privacy and independence. You know that the next stage may be nursing care. Life becomes a waiting game. Some people call assisted living the 'waiting room for heaven.'

What can sustain us as we live out our lives in the present, and anticipate the future? Paul highlights five aspects of our condition.

The Pledge – the Guarantee

First, we have the firstfruits of the Spirit. The firstfruits was the beginning of the harvest, and the pledge that the full harvest would follow in due time. The Spirit is given to us as the pledge, the first installment, deposit, or down-payment of the fullness of time that is to come, when the Spirit will be poured out on all people. "The Spirit testifies with our spirit that we are God's children." (Romans 8:16)

Our Impatience

Secondly, we groan inwardly. We share with the rest of creation in bondage to decay and its pain. We groan over our physical frailty and mortality, and that of our loved ones. "Meanwhile we groan, longing to be clothed with our resurrection body... For while we are in this temporary, flimsy, material body we groan and are burdened." (2 Cor.5:2,4) We groan also over our sinful nature, which hinders us from behaving as we should. We groan over our errors and omissions, our short-temper and cowardice, our addictions and obsessions. We long for wholeness and the transformation of our condition.

Thirdly, we wait eagerly for our adoption as sons, the redemption of our bodies. We have already been adopted and redeemed in Christ, but those promises won't be fully realized until our bodies have been redeemed in glory. We wait eagerly, and impatiently for fresh energy, new eyes, ears, internal organs, and limbs. We want to feel young again.

Our double hope

Fourthly, in this hope we were saved. We have been saved in Christ and we have experienced liberation from guilt, forgiveness and acceptance. "Yet we remain only half-saved. For we have not yet been saved from the out-pouring of God's judgment at the last day, nor have the final vestiges of sin in our human personality been eradicated. So we are saved in hope of our total liberation. This double hope looks to the future and to things which, being future, are so far unseen. For *hope that is seen*, having been realized in our experience, *is no hope at all. Who hopes for what he already has?* Instead, *we hope for what we do not have.*"[2]

Just because we do not have it now, does not mean that we will not experience it later. Despair is the belief that things can't change, and all is eventually lost. Hope is to believe that, with Christ our hope, time changes everything. We will not spend the rest of our lives in the waiting room. Some day, we believe, we will leave this earth and travel to our eternal destination.

---

[2] Stott, op. cit., 243

Fifthly, we wait for it patiently, that is, for the fulfillment of our hope. "For we are confident in God's promises that the firstfruits will be followed by the harvest, bondage by freedom, decay by renewal, and labor pains by the birth of the new world. This whole section is a notable example of what it means to be living 'in between times', present difficulty and future destiny, between the already and the not yet, between sufferings and glory."[3] In this tension the Christian waits, waits eagerly, with keen expectation, but also waits patiently, enduring the present stressfulness of life. Waiting eagerly, and waiting patiently is the balance required of us.

The need for balance

"Yet it is hard to keep this balance. Some Christians over-emphasize the call to patience. They lack enthusiasm and lapse into lethargy, apathy and pessimism. They have forgotten God's promises, and are guilty of unbelief. Others grow impatient of waiting. They are so carried away with enthusiasm that they almost try to force God's hand. They are determined to experience now even what is not available yet."[4] They are not prepared to undertake the rigors of the journey but want to arrive before they have departed. They are like children who are always asking, "Are we there yet? How long before we arrive?" Their impatience is a form of presumption. They want to rush God's timetable because they are not willing to be patient.

---

[3] Ibid.

[4] Ibid.

Samuel Beckitt's play, *Waiting for Godot*, depicts two men who spend two days waiting for Godot to meet them. He does not appear, despite his assurances that he will arrive. The play has multiple interpretations, but one is that Godot stands for God, who promises to come but lets us down. This is the attitude of unbelief. Faith believes that God has come in Christ and will return for us.

Be ready

Jesus told us that the kingdom of heaven is like ten virgins who took their lamps and went out to meet the bridegroom. The bridegroom was a long time in coming and they fell asleep. When he arrived those who had oil for their lamps and were ready for him, went into the wedding banquet. Those who did not were excluded. "Therefore, keep watch, because you do not know the day or the hour." (Matt.25:1-13)

Many a time I have ministered to those whose loved ones have met untimely deaths. They were shocked at the suddenness of it, and their unpreparedness for it. Yet, everyone knows that such a day will come. Their unwillingness to face their mortality and their failure to put their affairs in order for their survivors is evidence of their lack of faith, hope and love.

Jesus said, "Be dressed ready for service and keep your lamps burning, like men waiting for your master to return, so that when he comes and knocks they can immediately open the door for him. It will be good for those servants whose master finds them watching when he comes. I tell you the truth, he will dress himself to serve, will have them recline at table and will come and wait on them. It will be good for those servants whose master finds them ready, even if he comes in the second or third watch of the night. But understand this: If the owner of the house had known at what hour the thief was coming, he would not have let his house be broken into. You also must be ready, because the Son of Man will come at an hour when you do not expect him." (Luke 12:35-40)

How can we wait eagerly *and* patiently? By knowing the reasons for the hope in which we are saved. By being prepared for that day. What do you need to do to prepare?

16

PRAYER IN THE SPIRIT

"The Spirit helps us in our weakness. We do not know what we ought to pray for, but the Spirit himself intercedes for us with groans that words cannot express. And he who searches our hearts knows the mind of the Spirit, because the Spirit intercedes for the saints in accordance with God's will." (Romans 8:26,27)

There are many times in life when, because of our limited understanding of our situation, our ignorance of our condition, our tendency to self-deception, an awareness of our shortcomings, and the overwhelming problems confronting us, when everything seems to be against us, that we do not know what we ought to pray for. When we attempt to pray about our situation we are unsure whether to pray for deliverance, a miracle, a windfall, remission, a change in the behavior and attitudes of others, or whether we ought to pray only for strength and courage to endure whatever life has in store for us. We do not know what we ought to pray for. We do not know what is best for us, what is right for us, and we may pray for the wrong thing. We can be so confused and frustrated, so depressed and discouraged, that we cannot get the words out. We get tongue-tied and we are tempted to give up. We have prayed, and prayed, and nothing different seems to happen. Prayer becomes an exercise of the will, a self-centered obsession with our problems, a form of spiritual worrying rather than prayer in the Spirit.

Paul's thorn in the flesh

St. Paul speaks out of personal experience. He was given a thorn in the flesh, a messenger of Satan, to torment him. "Three times I pleaded with the Lord to take it away from me. But he said to me, 'My grace is sufficient for you, for my power is made perfect in weakness.' Therefore I will boast all the more gladly about my weaknesses, so that Christ's power may rest on me." (2 Corinthians 12:7-9)

The apostle was in trouble because of his weakness, his thorn in the flesh; and he acts in a very natural way in terms of human reason. He felt that this would cripple his work, put a limit upon his efficiency, so he prays three times for the Lord to remove it. But the Lord tells him that he is praying the wrong prayer. God was not going to deliver him from his problem. Then he begins to look at his situation in another manner. He begins to see that the Lord can accomplish more through his weakness that he could through his strength. He could not glory in his accomplishments, but in his weaknesses and God's grace, to enable him to have the strength to carry on.

We are prone to take the easy way out in our prayers. Our default position in prayer is for the removal of obstacles in front of us, or in us, so that we can sail straight forward to fulfill our agendas. But God may wish us to pray about some other way we should proceed. He may wish us to wait, to be patient, to endure, to be still and listen.

In Psalm 77 the writer was complaining in his sufferings.

> I cried out to God for help;
> I cried out to God to hear me.
> When I was in distress, I sought the Lord……
> Has God forgotten to be merciful?
> Has he in anger withheld his compassion?

Circumstances were against him. He is jealous of the serene and healthy lives of others, so he begins to blame God. Then he pulls himself together: "And I said, It is my own weakness," meaning that he should not be saying such things, that he was speaking foolishly. So instead of continuing to harbor such thoughts he says, "I will remember the years of the right hand of the Most High." In other words, he begins to remind himself of God's faithfulness in the past. Before we rush thoughtlessly into prayer we need to examine what God is doing in our lives, and not let an obsession with our weakness control us. It is better to acknowledge that we do not know what we ought to pray for. Do not be afraid or shamed to admit our lack of direction.

Paul does this in Philippians 1. He is in prison and using the opportunity of confinement to write his famous letters to the churches and to witness to his fellow-prisoners and the whole palace guard. He recognizes that what has happened to him has served to advance the gospel, for Christ is preached. Yet he does not know whether Christ would be better exalted by his life or by his death. He does not know what to pray for: "If I am to go on living in the body, this will mean fruitful labor for me. Yet what shall I choose? I do not know! I am torn between the two: I desire to depart and be with Christ, which is better by far; but it is more necessary for you that I remain in the body. Convinced of this, I know that I will remain, and I will continue with all of you for your progress and joy in the faith." (Philippians 1:22-25)

Perplexity in prayer

At first he is in difficulties as to what to pray for. He was possibly suffering ill-health, and had become old before his time. What shall he pray for? Shall he pray to the Lord to take him out of it all, to be with Christ, which is far better? So much seemed to argue in that direction. But then he remembers that it would be better for the Philippians that he should remain alive, that he might still teach, and guide, and help them. He does not know what the disposition of his case will be. He does not know what to pray for. In such a case it is better that we should acknowledge the perplexity and take it to God, tell him that we do not know, and leave it entirely in his hands. That is far wiser than forcing ourselves to a decision, or rushing to offer a prayer that seems to us to be natural.

Even Jesus experienced this challenge. "Now is my heart troubled and what shall I say? Father, save me from this hour? No, it was for this very reason I came to this hour." (John 12:27) In his time of human weakness, when his heart is troubled, he asks, "What shall I pray? Shall I ask the Father to save me from this hour?" Instead of taking the easy route by praying that he might be spared suffering and the Cross, he asked for strength to endure it.

We may fail to find the words to express our present dilemma. The Spirit comes to our aid and intercedes on our behalf. God knows exactly what is happening in our hearts. He knows all about our fears, our anxieties, our hopes, our desires. He understands us better than we understand ourselves. "Now I know in part; then I shall know fully, even as I am fully known." (1 Corinthians 13:12) "And he who searches our hearts knows the mind of the Spirit, because the Spirit intercedes for the saints in accordance with God's will." (Romans 8:27) We are being assured that the Spirit comes alongside us, takes up our worries and begins to act on our behalf with in us. This is the will of God for us, it is part of God's plan. God allows us to be tried, he allows things to take their course, even when they are difficult for us. But he also sends his Spirit to act on our behalf, to help us in our difficulties.

"God's Spirit is right alongside helping us along. If we don't know how or what to pray, it doesn't matter. He does our praying in and for us, making prayer out of our wordless sighs, our aching groans. He knows us far better than we know ourselves, knows our pregnant condition, and keeps us present before God." (*The Message*)

Prayer in the Spirit is resting in that assurance, and knowing that God is working for us and in us at all times.

17

WORKING FOR OUR GOOD

"And we know that in all things God works for the good of those who love him, who have been called according to his purpose." (Romans 8:28 NIV) "And we know that all things work together for good to those who love God."[Or] "works together with those who love him to bring about what is good – with those who are called according to his purpose." (NIV margin – other manuscripts) "And we know that all that happens to us is working for our good if we love God and are fitting into his plans." (LB)

This verse is a life-preserver to those who are going through a storm of suffering. Yet I must add a caveat: You must know how or when to say it to someone who is suffering. It must not be said glibly or casually as though it is a mantra which will solve all problems. Remember that Job's friends said many true things to Job but they were said insensitively, and untimely. This saying can be used as a hammer to hurt people further if it is used as a neat panacea for suffering.

However we translate this famous verse, the stumbling block, or the kicker, that seems to either stick in the throat that we can't swallow, or the reassurance that comforts us in the midst of suffering is, 'in all things', i.e. that nothing happens by chance, that everything that happens to us is part of God's purpose for good, what believers two or three hundred years ago would call *Providence.* This challenges us to reconcile acute suffering with our belief in an all-powerful, all-knowing, and all-loving God.

Holmes Rolston, III, Templeton prize-winner for his work in the relationship between science and Christianity, tells the story of family suffering. "On graduation from Hampden-Sydney Seminary in the mid-1890's, Rolston's paternal grandfather, Holmes Rolston I, had been called to his first pastorate in Horton, West Virginia. There he had worked among the hardened men of the Allegheny Mountain lumber camps. [He] took with him to Horton his new wife, Jacqueline Campbell.

Life in the lumber camps of West Virginia was harsh. There were no churches yet established in that part of the county. The lumbermen were constantly drunk and fighting. The wooden shack in which the couple lived was cold in winter and full of flies in summer. Despite the hardships, the young pastor and his wife devoted themselves to each other and to their work creating a church community.

In late summer they celebrated the birth of their first child, Archibald Campbell Rolston. The celebration was brief. Archibald was sickly, barely clinging to life from the moment of his birth. In the oppressive August heat the infant never seemed to gain much strength. The lumber camp was a long way from any hospital and his parents watched helplessly as the color of their son's cheeks paled. Archibald died in the Horton home less than three weeks after his birth. [So many women have suffered through nine months of pregnancy, and the labor of birth, only to see their baby die. One of my sisters-in-law suffered losing three babies in this way!]

Determined the infant should have a proper burial, Rolston's grandfather put his son's body in the back of the one-horse buggy and set out in the early morning for his brother-in-law's New Providence Church [in the Shenandoah Valley of Virginia]. He rode alone for seventy miles, stopping only to rest and water the horse. Upon arrival at New Providence, the pastor found his anguish magnified. His sister-in-law's own firstborn, a young girl of two weeks name Jacqueline Campbell Wilson, had died the day before his own child. The two Campbell sisters had each lost their firstborn within twenty-four hours. The infants were buried side by side in the New Providence cemetery with a single tombstone recording the double tragedy. Intense suffering seemed to be part of every family story. Acceptance of this suffering as part of God's order seemed to be a demand of faith.

....Part of what had driven Charles Darwin from his faith was his despair at the amount of suffering, misery, and waste the supposedly benign creator had permitted on earth. Having lost his mother to a tumor when he was a child and his favorite daughter, Annie, to a painful illness when she was only nine, Darwin had cause far beyond the morphology of Galapagos finches to embrace natural selection over divine creation. [This issue of suffering is central to psyche of many who have lost their faith in a loving God. Most atheists have ceased to believe in God because of the suffering they experience. They take their anger out on God by rejecting him.]

Soul-making

...To Darwin's key question about the purpose of all suffering Rolston expanded on the [teaching] offered by second-century theologian Irenaeus of Lyon. Irenaeus had pointed out how much was to be gained from suffering. One had only to look past the immediate hardship to see the later spiritual gain. Suffering was 'soul-making,' providing opportunities to develop the Christian virtues.... The enlivening truth Rolston had learned...during countless hours of counseling his parishioners, and through listening to numerous family stories about the hardships faithfully endured by his southern ancestors was that life survives, and even flourishes, in the midst of its perpetual perishing....Life is suffering, life is suffering through to something higher. [Many people who experience suffering drop out of church life. They simply disappear. They have never learned how to understand the purpose of suffering in their lives. Others return and are prayed for and loved through their suffering. They develop their souls.]

...To be chosen by God is not to be protected from suffering. It is a call to suffer and to be delivered as one passes through it.... So far from making the world absurd, suffering is a key to the whole....The capacity to suffer through to joy is a supreme emergent and an essence of Christianity...Life is gathered up in the midst of its throes, a blessed tragedy, lived in grace through a besetting storm....Christ lived a life of sacrificial suffering so that humanity could reach something higher....Christ's death on the cross was necessary for the possibility of human redemption from sin."[1]

Purpose in Suffering

Believing that "in all things God works for the good of those who love him, who have been called according to his purpose" requires believing that there is a purpose in suffering. Purposeless suffering is a soul-destroyer. We have to believe that there is a purpose, and that that purpose is 'for the good of those who love God.' We may not see or understand that purpose, but we have to have faith that such a purpose exists, and that good will eventually come out of it. God is ceaselessly, energetically and purposefully active on our behalf to make good come out of our suffering.

The key is our attitude to, and trust in, God. We have to believe that God is good and that he is love. We cannot love God otherwise. If we believe that God is good and that God is love, then we can endure anything.

Jeanie Miley writes about a woman who was a cancer patient getting treatment at M.D. Anderson Cancer Center in Houston. 'Over the course of the study of Job, she had sat at the very edge of the crowd. Now, she wore the telltale turban. She had become pale and weak, and yet there was a light to her eyes, and a brilliance to her smile, that dazzled me. "Don't stop affirming the goodness of God," she said to me, and then she simply knocked me over with her simple affirmation of faith. "You know, I'm not going to live," she

---

[1] *Saving Creation: Nature and Faith in the Life of Holmes Rolston III*, Christopher J. Preston, Trinity University Press, San Antonio, 2009, 216-222

continued, "and I'm at the bottom, but what I have discovered is that it is people who have been to the bottom, who learn that God is there, right there with us, and that God is love.'"[2]

Jesus said, "My sheep listen to my voice; I know them, and they follow me. I give them eternal life and they shall never perish; no one can snatch them out of my Father's hand. I and the Father are one." (John 10:27-29)

Life is a battle for the victory of hope over despair

If we believe in the love of God, and that life is a calling to fulfill God's purpose, then we will see all things as opportunities for soul-making. How we handle the events of our lives, whether they be pain or pleasure, contributes to our spiritual formation, to our spiritual maturity. "Endure hardship with us, like a good soldier of Christ Jesus." (2 Timothy 2:3) Life is a battle for the victory of hope over despair. In the battle we will be wounded. But however badly we have been injured, we must continue to believe that we will be healed and made whole. That is God's ultimate purpose for us as we trust in him.

My grandfather fought in the trenches of World War I and returned home with very little in the way of physical wounds. Yet emotionally he had suffered unspeakable horrors. What purpose was in it? He died at age 46 before I was born. His life affected my mother, and ultimately, myself. Perhaps it contributed to my entering the ministry.

---

[2] *Sitting Strong: Wrestling with the Ornery God*, Jeanie Miley, Smyth & Helwys, Macon, 2006, 31

Something good may have come out of his suffering but only two generations removed.

Jesus said, "I am the good shepherd. The good shepherd lays down his life for the sheep. The hired hand is not the shepherd who owns the sheep. So when he sees the wolf coming, he abandons the sheep and runs away. Then the wolf attacks the flock and scatters it. The man runs away because he is a hired hand and cares nothing for the sheep. I am the good shepherd; I know my sheep and my sheep know me – just as the Father knows me and I know the Father – and I lay down my life for the sheep." (John 10:11-15)

If this God in Christ, suffers and dies for us, to fulfill his purpose for us, then we can be assured that he is good and that he loves us enough to work through all things for our good.

Help to understand the things that happen – in the will of God - and to give hope

In the Amelia Plantation Chapel *Lenten Meditations for 2011,* Iris Jacobsen wrote, "Sometimes bad things happen to good people, sometimes things that should be so simple are not. Sometimes we plan and we hope about how things will go, but they simply do not turn out that way.... All of my life I have heard and respected spiritual people who have talked about events being the will of God. This poem has helped me to understand the things that have happened and given me hope; perhaps it will help you as well.

The will of God will never take you
Where the grace of God cannot keep you,
Where the arms of God cannot support you,
Where the riches of God cannot supply your needs,
Where the power of God cannot endow you.

The will of God can never take you
Where the Spirit of God cannot work through you,
Where the wisdom of God cannot teach you,
Where the army of God cannot protect you,
Where the hands of God cannot mold you.

The will of God will never take you
Where the love of God cannot enfold you,
Where the mercies of God cannot sustain you,
Where the peace of God cannot calm your fears,
Where the authority of God cannot overrule for you.

The will of God will never take you
Where the comfort of God cannot dry your tears,
Where the Word of God cannot feed you,
Where the miracles of God cannot be done for you,
Where the omnipresence of God cannot find you.

...God will help us endure, grow and win the victory over the things that happen in our lives. That is the will of God."

Ray David Glenn suddenly lost his beautiful, young wife, and mother of his son, to a brain tumor. He went through an intense period of grieving that tested him. I will never forget him sharing his experience of that time with a group of us, and concluding with these words of the Heidelberg Catechism, which I had never heard before.

> **"What is your only comfort in life and death?**
>
> That I am not my own, but belong – body and soul, in life and death – to my faithful Savior Jesus Christ.
>
> He has fully paid for all my sins with his precious blood, and has set me free from the tyranny of the devil.
> He also watches over me in such a way that not a hair can fall from my head without the will of my Father in heaven:
> in fact, all things must work together for my salvation.
>
> Because I belong to him, Christ, by his Holy Spirit, assures me of eternal life and makes me wholeheartedly willing and ready from now on to live for him."

Only a person who has suffered can fully affirm that faith and appreciate that comfort.

18

FOR OUR GOOD?

"And we know that in all things God works for the good of those who love him, who have been called according to his purpose." (Romans 8:28)

How can God work for the good of those who love him in the midst of tragedy? How can trials be occasions of joyfulness? How can the testing of our faith produce endurance so that we may be mature and complete, lacking in nothing? (James 1:2-4)

James Bryan Smith in *The Good and Beautiful God*, relates about when the doctors told he and his wife that the little girl she had been carrying for eight months had a rare chromosomal disorder that would likely cause her to die at birth. Up to that point in his life nothing terrible had happened to him. From painting his child's nursery he had to plan her funeral. He asked, "How does a Christian, one who believes in the goodness of God, respond to something so tragic and heartbreaking?"

Their daughter, Madelaine survived the birth, but weighed only a few pounds, had a heart defect, was deaf and could not keep food down. They were told she would not live more than a year or two. One day a pastor whom he had known for years took him to lunch. While Jim was in the middle of eating his salad he asked, “Who sinned, Jim, you or your wife?” Jim replied, “Excuse me...what do you mean?” He said, “Well, one or both of you must have sinned at some point to have caused this to happen.” Job’s comforters again! If Romans 8:28 is true then you must not be loving God if something bad is happening to you!

Crass Comments

Madeline lived for just over two years, and then her little body gave up the fight. Over those two years, and the year after, people said some outrageously ignorant and tactless things to them. During the viewing the night before Madelaine’s funeral a woman said to his wife, “It’s okay honey, you can have another child.” The comments that bothered him the most were the theological ones explaining what God was up to in all this. “Well, I am sure the Lord had a reason for this,” several people said. “I guess God just wanted her in heaven more than he wanted her here,” said another. “Sometimes children are too beautiful for this earth,” said yet another.

The pastor who asked the question, “Who sinned?” was operating from the most prevalent narrative about God among Christians: “God is an angry judge. If you do well, you will be blessed; if you sin, you will be punished.” A study conducted by Baylor University concluded that this is the way most conservative Christians think about God. His daughter, however had not sinned and caused this disease. What possible sin could his wife or he have done that God would force a small child to suffer for it?

Jesus encountered a man who was born blind, and was asked a question by his disciples, "Rabbi, who sinned, this man or his parents, that he was born blind?" Jesus answered, "Neither this man nor his parents sinned; he was born blind so that God's works might be revealed in him." (John 9:2,3) Jesus was making it clear that there is no correlation between someone's sin and his infirmity. Instead Jesus healed the man. If he believed that the man's blindness was a fair and just punishment for his sins he could have walked away. Instead Jesus healed the blind man and so revealed the power of God.

Opportunity to do God's Work

Merrill Tenney concludes, "Jesus refused to accept either alternative suggested by the disciples' question. He looked on the man's plight, not as retribution for some offense committed either by his parents or himself, but as an opportunity to do God's work. Jesus did not consider the blindness as punishment or as a matter of irrational chance; it was a challenge to manifest God's healing power in the man's life."

Jim Smith believes, that we never know, in this life, why anything happens to any of us. There seems to be little justice in this life. St. Augustine tells us that one day we will understand:

"When we come to Judgment Day not only will the judgments passed there seem to be most just, but all the judgments of God from the beginning will be likewise clearly fair. Then too it will also become clear how just the judgment of God is in causing so many – in fact, almost all – of his judgments to evade men's grasp of understanding.

Those who have faith will not fail to realize that such hidden judgments are just." If Augustine were his pastor he would say, "We cannot know these things here and now – they are beyond our grasp. But I believe that one day it will all become clear. One day you will fully understand why God allowed your daughter to be born with a birth defect and why she died young, and I believe that when you understand why, you will see that God was not only just, but good."

God is Good – all the time

Jesus said that his Father was good. Jesus also refused to affirm the idea that external rewards and punishments are given by God on the basis of our good or bad works. Rain falls on the good and the bad. Sometimes we pray for rain (for our crops), and sometimes we pray that it will not rain (for our picnic). Both good and bad people get rained on, whether they want to or not. (Matthew 5:45) Jesus faced suffering, rejection and alienation, and the people jeered at him as he hung on the cross, questioning whether God was really with him. And Jesus believed. And he believes for us. He believes even when we cannot. He prays even when we cannot. It is a gift from the Holy Spirit to believe in a God who is good even when things look bleak.

A year after Madelaine died Jim Smith reflected on the pain of hearing the news from the doctors, the countless sleepless nights on hospital floors, and the dark, rainy day, when they placed her body in the earth. He turned to God and said, without thinking, "Maybe it would have been better if she had never been born."

That was when he received one of the clearest experiences of God responding to him that he had ever had in his life. On that day, at that moment, a little voice penetrated his mind, the voice of a little girl, a voice he had never heard but immediately recognized as Madelaine's. "Daddy, you should never say that. If I had never been born, I would not be here now. I am so happy here in heaven, and one day you and Mom and Jacob will come and see me, and we will live forever together. And there is more good that has happened because of me that you can't see now but will one day understand."

A girl named Hope

Two years after Madelaine's death Jim's wife became pregnant again. For eight months they lived with a lot of anxiety, mixed with a little faith. When it came time to have the final sonogram, their hearts were in their throats, bracing for bad news. The technician, who did not know their story, kept saying things they loved to hear: "Perfect hands....perfect heart...your baby looks just perfect. Do you want to know the gender?" They said yes. "It's a little girl." They both smiled. "What are you going to name her?" she asked. At the very same moment they said, "Hope."

We can grow much more through our trials than through our successes. They can work for our good, if we allow them. God has his purpose. It may not be seen in our lifetime, or on this earth, but it will be fulfilled. In the meantime we are sustained by the knowledge that God suffers with us in all things. He gives us the strength to endure, even to experience joy, and above all he gives us hope if we trust in him, that he is good and that he is love.

Guide de Bres (1522-67) author of the Belgic Confession (1561), wrote this letter to his wife shortly before he was executed for his Reformed faith by the Spanish authorities:

"Your grief and anguish, troubling me in the midst of my joy and gladness, are the cause of my writing you this present letter. I most earnestly pray you not to be grieved beyond measure....If the Lord has wished us to live together longer, He could certainly caused it to be so...Let His good will be done, then, and let that suffice for all reason....I pray you, my dear and faithful companion, to be glad with me, and to thank the good God for what He is doing, for He does nothing but what is altogether right and good.....

I am shut up in the strongest and wretchedest of dungeons, so dark and gloomy that it goes by the name of the Black Hole. I can get but little air, and that of the foulest. I have on my hands and feet heavy irons which are a constant torture, galling the flesh even to my poor bones. But notwithstanding all, my God fails not to make good His promise, and to comfort my heart, and to give me a most blessed content."[1]

---

[1] Quoted in Cornelius Plantinga Jr., *A Place to Stand*, Grand Rapids: Board of Publications of the Christian Reformed Church, 1981, p.35

19

THERE IS A DIVINE PURPOSE

"We know that in all things God works for the good of those who love him, who have been called according to his purpose." (Romans 8:28)

Do you believe that life has a purpose, or do you believe that life is random? Belief in a divine purpose to our lives, to the world, to all creation and its history, is the teaching of the Holy Scriptures. Yet this belief is dismissed by secular writers who argue for the essentially random and contingent nature of the evolutionary process. Stephen Jay Gould (1941-2002) wrote that it is pointless to talk about purpose, historical inevitability, or direction. "We are the accidental result of an unplanned process....the fragile result of an enormous concatenation of improbabilities, not the predictable product of any definite process."[1]

The notion of purpose is not a scientific term. Science can only observe, describe, and draw conclusions. It cannot import from theology (or metaphysics) a belief in a divine

---

[1] Alister McGrath, *A Fine-Tuned Universe*, 189

ordainer of purpose. But neither can it deny its possibility. There is no reason why the evolutionary process could not be compatible with the achievement of purpose on the part of God. Theists are free to insist that their belief "provides an equally rational and plausible explanation which may ultimately prove to be the *best* explanation."[2]

The Great Theme

St. Paul consistently refers to God's purpose in creation and salvation. "This is indeed the great theme of the whole of the Bible. The Bible is a collection of books, but it has only one great theme; and this theme concerning God's purpose runs through it from beginning to end. The Bible declares that purpose and shows its unfolding in history. I make bold to assert that a person cannot really understand the Bible and its teaching unless he understands something about this teaching concerning God's purpose. It is implicit in the whole teaching of the Bible and if we fail to see this unifying principle in it – in the plain teaching, in the history, in everything – then we have a wrong or very inadequate view of the teaching of the Bible. So here we are dealing with something that is basic, not only to the understanding of salvation, but even to an understanding of the Bible itself as the Word of God."[3]

Life is not the random mess which it may sometimes appear. God, in all things, is working toward our supreme good. The story of Joseph is an example of this. His brothers sold him into slavery in Egypt but he rose to be prime minister to Pharoah. When his brothers came looking for food in the

---

[2] McGrath, op.cit. 196

[3] D. Martyn Lloyd-Jones, *Romans*, 207

midst of a famine he said to them, "You intended to harm me, but God intended it for good....the saving of many lives." (Genesis 50:20) Jeremiah wrote in God's name a letter to the Jews in Babylonian exile after the catastrophic destruction of Jerusalem: "I know the plans I have for you, declares the LORD, "plans to prosper you and not to harm you, plans to give you hope and a future." (Jeremiah 29:11)

My Memoir

How deeply do you believe that you have been called according to God's purpose? As you look back on your life, do you see any rhyme or reason, any plan or purpose in it? The person who sees his life in terms of a divine destiny, the fulfillment of a calling, a spiritual vocation, experiences confidence in the present and in the future. Many years ago I wrote a memoir of my life entitled *Divine Destiny: Discovering Meaning and Purpose in Life*. I wrote it to help people who have a struggle making sense of their lives. Many feel that there is no value and purpose to their lives. In the memoir (still unpublished), I used incidents in my life to illustrate the thesis that there is a pattern to life. My life would be incomprehensible if there weren't such a pattern. How could my wanderings from New Zealand to England, to Massachusetts, Florida, Texas and then back to Florida make any sense at all except by the Providence of God?

Is there any sense, any reason, for the twists and turns of life? Is it all a matter of aimless choices, that result in labyrinthine confusion? How do we know if there is meaning and purpose to life?

William Cullen Bryant's famous poem, ***TO A WATERFOWL*** sheds some light on the question.

There is a power whose care
Teaches thy way along that
pathless coast, -
The desert and illimitable air, -
Lone wandering, but not lost.

All day thy wings have fanned,
At that far height, the cold, thin
atmosphere,
Yet stoop not, weary, to the
welcome land,
Though the dark night is near.

And soon that toil shall end;
Soon shalt thou find a summer
home, and rest,
And scream among thy fellows;
reeds shall bend,
Soon, o'er thy sheltered nest.

Thou'rt gone, the abyss of heaven
Hath swallowed up thy form; yet,
on my heart
Deeply hath sunk the lesson thou
hast given,
And shall not soon depart.

He who, from zone to zone,
Guides through the boundless sky

thy certain flight,
In the long way that I must tread
alone,
Will lead my steps aright.

The waterfowl seems lost, but there is a Power whose care teaches his way along the pathless coast. We may seem "lone wandering", but we are not lost. The lesson of the waterfowl is that

He who from zone to zone,
Guides through the boundless sky thy certain flight,
In the long way that I must tread alone
Will lead my steps aright.

The autopilot of migratory birds

There is built into migratory birds an autopilot that guides them to where they should go. No doubt there are choices to be made, weather to adjust to, food to find, but the course is set. Each bird has a different guidance system, directing it to a unique destination, but it is not alone. There is a Power who cares to the extent that not a sparrow falls to the ground without his notice. The structure of Nature, the way physics and biology works, is the means through which God's purposes are fulfilled. There is no incompatibility between God and the Nature, the Bible and Science.

What is so for the birds of the air, is also true for us? "Are you not much more valuable than they?" (Matt.6:26) What if God has built into us a guidance system that directs us along life's journey? Can we look back and discern where he has led us? If so, is not our faith increased, as we see that our lives contain a divine purpose? What has seemed from time to time a meaningless meandering, becomes an appointment with destiny. Nothing is insignificant, as each incident leads on to another choice, another turn in the road.

Discovering God's pattern

This is not a recipe for determinism. Our need to make choices does not weaken God's powerful sovereignty. We cannot know the end from the beginning. Our choices are truly free. We do not know the script. We are not being manipulated into thinking we are making free choices when we are not. But through all our choices God is working out his purposes. As Paul put it, "continue to work out your salvation with fear and trembling, for it is God who works in you to will and to act according to his good purpose." (Phil.2:12,13) We are working out our future, making terribly important decisions that matter. God also is working out his purpose in us so that we will choose his will. It is both/and, not either/or. This approach makes life full of meaning and purpose. There is a pattern to discover. We can see all of life as worthwhile. Nothing that we do is wasted. Events take on heightened meaning. Coincidences become providential happenings. Retrospective reflection unearths a treasury of connections that we had not imagined before.

We are called according to God's purpose. We are called to fulfill a divine destiny. Our lives are valuable in God's sight. He has invested himself in them. Before the universe was even created God had a purpose and a destiny for us. "For he chose us in Christ before the creation of the world to be holy and blameless in his sight." (Ephesians 1:3) Let us thank him for it by seeking to serve him all our days.

20

CALLED AND CHOSEN

"For those God foreknew he also predestined to be conformed to the likeness of his Son, that he might be the firstborn among many brothers. And those he predestined, he also called; those he called, he also justified; those he justified, he also glorified." (Romans 8:29,30 *NIV*)

"God knew what he was doing from the very beginning. He decided from the outset to shape the lives of those who love him along the same lines as the life of his Son. The Son stands first in the line of humanity he restored. We see the original and intended shape of our lives there in him. After God made that decision of what his children should be like, he followed it up by calling people by name. After he called them by name, he set them on a solid basis with himself. And then, after getting them established, he stayed with them to the end, gloriously completing what he had begun." (Romans 8:29,30 *The Message*)

God has a plan for the world and for us individually. God has had a plan since before the beginning of time. It has now been revealed to us through the appearing of our Savior, Christ Jesus, who has destroyed death and has brought life and immortality to light through the gospel. (2 Timothy 1:9,10)

What is God's plan for us?

That plan of salvation is to deliver us from the realm of death and condemnation, to redeem us from sin: frustration, fear, despair and failure, to make us into the likeness of Christ, the fullness of humanity in the kingdom of heaven. To that end he calls us to faith in Christ, he invites us to follow him, and he gives us the grace to accept that invitation. He makes it possible for us to believe, to respond to his call to us. He breaks through our ignorance, our reluctance, our blindness, to enable us to have faith. "For it is by grace you have been saved, through faith – and this not from yourselves, it is the gift of God – not by works, so that no one can boast." (Ephesians 2:8,9)

God's sovereign will and our free will

God knew what we would do in response to his call, but we did not know. There is therefore no loss of responsibility on our part, or any compulsion on God's part. God is sovereign in his will and he gives us freedom to make choices. Christianity is a relationship between a loving and just God, who is fulfilling his eternal purpose of creation and salvation, and finite, fallen men and women who have been given the liberty and autonomy to make moral choices. This belief, in a balance between God's action and human response, is different from secular Darwinians who are determinists, or devotees of other religions who are fatalists.

Chosen to serve

The Bible tells the story of God calling and choosing people to privilege and service. Abraham was called and chosen to become a blessing to many. "I will make your name great and you will be a blessing....and all peoples on earth will be blessed through you." (Genesis 12:2,3) God selects some to reach all. He chooses Israel to be a light to the nations. His choice falls on the tribe of Judah from which the Messiah comes. Jesus chooses the twelve disciples, and then the seventy, to proclaim the kingdom of God. He chooses Moses and all the prophets and apostles to fulfill his purpose. He is still calling and choosing people to be his disciples and messengers. He is still choosing the children of Abraham, who live by faith, to be a blessing through their service. God's choice, and election of people is not for exclusion, to give them a sense of being superior to others who are lost. They are chosen to bring a wider blessing to others. They are chosen to be earlier entrants into the kingdom of God, but only so that others may later enter themselves. Those who first believed are to be followed by those who come in later. "In Christ we were chosen having been predestined according to the plan of him who works out everything in conformity with the purpose of his will in order that we, who were the first to hope in Christ might be for the praise of his glory." (Ephesians 1:11,12)

My humanly, inexplicable call

To be called and chosen for this privileged service is a cause for gratitude and for accountability. As I look back on my life I am humbled and grateful for the privilege of knowing Christ, of being called and chosen to enjoy God's grace of salvation. There is no earthly reason why I should have become a Christian, or been called into the ordained ministry. There is no human explanation why a boy from a small country town in New Zealand should have studied theology at Durham University in England, been ordained into the Gospel ministry in St. Paul's Cathedral, London, on September 29, 1967 and chosen to serve in one of the most famous churches of that city (All Souls, Langham Place), under a world-renowned preacher (John Stott), where he met a Southern belle from South Carolina who became his wife. I came from no devout family. No one that I knew of in my family had any living faith. No one prayed. No one read their Bible. My parents were not regular church goers. Yet God put a hunger in my heart for eternal life, and questions in my mind about the meaning and purpose of life. My parents sent me to Sunday School, and I was confirmed. God gave me a minister who preached the Gospel and taught from the Bible. God gave me a desire to read the Scriptures, and other Christian books. My minister gave me books from his library: biographies of missionaries, and other devotional classics. I went away to Christian camps in the summer, not because my parents wanted to send me – they had no idea what they were about. God gave me a thirst for Christian teaching and fellowship that, on looking back, was extraordinary. I am sure that my parents were worried about the interest I was exhibiting in my faith. What is amazing about it all is that, apart from my minister, and the local Anglican church, I was on my own. But I wasn't. God had a plan and purpose for my life that had taken hold of me. He knew what he was doing from the very beginning. He was shaping my life along the same lines as the life of His Son. He called me through the witness of a mission team in my church when I was fourteen years old. He set me on a solid basis with himself through my opening my life to the indwelling of Christ, who called me to become a blessing to others. God did all this in me. It was all because of his grace and mercy. I merely responded in faith.

The parallel lines

Here we see parallel lines of divine sovereignty and human freedom and responsibility. St. Bernard of Clairvaux famously quipped: "Take away free will and there would be nothing to save; take away grace and there would be nothing to save with."

We cannot save ourselves. Exhorting people to take responsibility for themselves without the provision of God's grace is worthless. Unless we open ourselves to God's call and respond to his invitation in faith, we cannot be blessed or be a blessing to others. There is no favoritism with God. There is no injustice or interference with human freedom. The Gospel is available to all people. God's sovereign purpose and human freedom are complementary truths. They are parallel lines, two poles of the magnet. Jesus said, "No one can come to me unless the Father who sent me draws him, and I will raise him up at the last day. It is written in the Prophets: 'They will all be taught by God.' Everyone who listens to the Father and learns from him comes to me." (John 6:44,45)

The mighty incentive

The practical application of knowing that you are called and chosen by the sovereign will of God is to strengthen you in God's service. You know that it is not entirely up to you. God has a stake in your life. He has a purpose to fulfill through you. He is doing his work. People who knew this truth did amazing things. The seventeenth century Puritans, like the Pilgrims who settled New England, believed that they were called and chosen. W.H. Griffith Thomas concluded his exposition of this doctrine with these words, "the realization that we are predestinated and elected to life is one of the mightiest incentives to true Christian living. It humbles pride by putting God first; it encourages faith by making God's grace real; it rebukes unbelief by reminding us of God's foresight and provision; it elicits earnestness by the consciousness of God's wonderful thought and love; and it emphasized holiness by the remembrance of what manner of persons we ought to be who are the subjects of this Divine and glorious purpose."[1]

[1] W.H. Griffith-Thomas, *The Principles of Theology*, London, Church Book Room Press, 1963, 257

21

GOD IS FOR US

"What, then, shall we say in response to this?" (Romans 8:31)

This is Paul's *peroration:* the concluding part of a speech in which there is a summing up and emphatic recapitulation.

St. Paul has been arguing that "in all things God works for the good of those who love him, who have been called according to his purpose." (Romans 8:28) God has a purpose to fulfill in and through us. We are called and chosen to do God's will. When our bodies are redeemed God will bring us to his glorious presence in his heavenly kingdom. That is our hope, for which we wait patiently in this life, despite our weakness. For our present sufferings, which we share with Christ, are not worth comparing with the glory that will be revealed in us. In response to all this, in light of this hope, this analysis of our salvation in Christ, what is there left to say? What can he add? He sums up his argument with a series of rhetorical questions, that contain within them unassailable logic.

"He hurls them into space, as it were, in a spirit of bold defiance. He challenges anybody and everybody, in heaven, earth, or hell, to answer them and to deny the truth which they contain. But there is no answer. For no-one and nothing can harm the people whom God has foreknown, predestined, called, justified and glorified."[1]

His first question is: "If God is for us, who can be against us?" (Romans 8:31)

If God is for us, then whatever is against us cannot prevail. We have to start with God being for us if we are to overcome anything that opposes us, anything that would diminish us, or seek to defeat and destroy us. All too often we begin with our enemy, that which is against us, rather than that which is for us. When we concentrate on the foe, we can easily be defeated. In military terms, we can be intimidated by the enemy. We have to know the enemy, but we must not allow the enemy to demoralize us. Morale is a key factor for our strength. We are to put on the full armor of God so that when the day of evil comes, we may be able to stand our ground. (Ephesians 6:13) This is the witness of all the saints of God.

What is it that comes against us, and seeks to defeat us? It may be illness or disease of any kind. I have a magnet with these words on it:

"What Cancer Cannot Take From Your Life
It cannot take away your faith, shatter your hope, or lessen your love.
It cannot destroy true friendship, invade the soul or take away eternal life.
It cannot conquer your spirit."

[1] John Stott, *Romans*, 254

What comes against us may be financial pressures, retirement plans, family problems, fear about the future, anxiety about change, concerns about actions of Congress, dismay about the direction of our country, apprehension about increased taxes and budget deficits, uncertainty about health care, or worry about our grandchildren. It may be the assault of a secular and immoral culture where nothing is sacred - talk show hosts, movies, authors, artists and comedians who spew out blasphemy, and academics who indoctrinate students into moral relativism and historical deconstruction. It may be doubts about our beliefs, whether there is any life after death, the immensity of the universe and our place in it, if Christ is the Son of God, if there is heaven and hell, if life has any eternal significance, if we have any value, or are we just whistling in the dark?

What discourages and depresses you?

What is it that is against your wellbeing, against your assurance, that discourages and depresses you? Is it questions about having any purpose to life? Is it the presence of people who are cruel, unkind and self-centered? Is it the prevalence of people who are indifferent to God, who dismiss your faith, who think that Christianity is for the weak-minded and deluded? Is it the existence of millions of people of other faiths or no faith? What is it that comes against you in the middle of the night, and fills you with despair?

The list is endless. All of us have fears that seek to control us. The devil schemes to tempt us to despair and disbelieve. We must resist him and all spirits that come against us. But how?

Why is God for us?

"If God is for us, who can be against us?" How can we know that God is for us? God is not *for* everybody. Many times God declares that he is *against* people and decadent societies. Nahum prophesied against the evils of Nineveh: "I am against you," declares the Lord Almighty. "I will burn up your chariots in smoke, and the sword will devour your young lions." (2:13) Jeremiah prophesied against Babylon: "See, I am against you, O arrogant one," declares the Lord Almighty, "for your day has come, the time for you to be punished." (50:31) Ezekiel prophesied, "This is what the Sovereign Lord says: 'I am against you, Pharoah king of Egypt, you great monster lying among your streams.'" (29:3) Tyre, Sidon and Edom come under the same condemnation for their evils. Even Israel is condemned for her disobedience, idolatry, and false leaders: "I will set my face against you so that you will be defeated by your enemies." (Lev.26:17) "Therefore this is what the Sovereign Lord says: Because of your false words and lying visions, I am against you, declares the Sovereign Lord." (Ezekiel 13:8)

But Paul confidently affirms that God is for us since, in Christ, God has called and chosen us to fulfill his purpose of redemption. By grace we are saved through faith. We can be assured that we are on God's side, if we are in Christ. We can do everything through Christ who gives us strength. (Phil.4:13) He stands alongside us to help us when we call upon him. The promises of Holy Scripture assure us of this truth.

"Then my enemies will turn back when I call for help.
By this I will know that God is for me." (Psalm 56:9)

"The Lord is with me; I will not be afraid.
What can man do to me?
The Lord is with me; he is my helper.
I will look in triumph on my enemies." (Ps.118:6,7)

"Raise the war cry, you nations, and be shattered!
Listen, all you distant lands.
Prepare for battle, and be shattered!
Prepare for battle, and be shattered!
Devise your strategy, but it will be thwarted;
propose your plan, but it will not stand,
for God is with us." (Isaiah 8:9,10)

"But the Lord is with me like a mighty warrior;
so my persecutors will stumble and not prevail.
They will fail and be thoroughly disgraced;
their dishonor will never be forgotten." (Jeremiah 20:11)

Life is a battle between good and evil, between hope and despair, between faith and doubt, between love of others and love of self, between humility and pride, between the Spirit of truth and the father of lies: the accuser of the saints. (Rev.12:10) But, because God has shown that he is for us in Christ, we can overcome the accuser, those who come against us, by the blood of the Lamb and the word of our testimony. (Rev.12:11) Therefore we must arm ourselves with knowledge of the power of the Cross and the word of the Gospel.

We must never allow ourselves to be demoralized by the powers of hell, no matter what medium it uses. If God is for us we believe we can never be finally defeated. “The race is not to the swift or the battle to the strong.” (Eccl.9:11) Victory is assured to those who trust in the Lord and keep the faith. No matter what the world may do to us, whatever the weakness of the flesh, whatever the assaults of the enemy, we will prevail, because God is for us in Christ. Even death has no ultimate hold over us, because death has been defeated in the resurrection of Jesus.

22

GOD'S PROMISE TO MEET OUR REAL NEEDS

"He who did not spare his own Son, but gave him up for us all – how will he not also, along with him, graciously give us all things?" (Romans 8:32)

What is your image of God? Do you see God as stingy or generous? Does he delight is giving you all good things, or does he withhold from you what you need? The good news of Jesus is that God did all that he could to meet our real needs. God demonstrated his astounding love for us by giving us his own Son, to die for us to redeem us, to pay for our sins, to live with us and through us. His purpose is that we might enjoy life in all its fullness through communion with him.

How can we possibly be sure that God will supply all that we need to live a full life? What are our needs anyway? There might be a debate about what we *really* need. Paul is not saying that God promises to meet all our wants. There is a big difference between wants and needs. Nor is Paul saying that we do not need to do anything to meet our basic needs. We have responsibility to provide for ourselves as best as we can.

Maslow's Hierarchy of Needs

Humanistic psychologist, Abraham Maslow developed a theory of the hierarchy of needs. He saw human beings' needs arranged like a ladder. The most basic needs, at the bottom, were physical — air, water, food, sleep. Then came safety needs — security, stability — followed by psychological, or social needs—for belonging, love, acceptance. Then came esteem needs — to feel achievement, status, responsibility, and reputation. At the top of it all were the self-actualizing needs — the need to fulfill oneself, to become all that one is capable of becoming. The basic needs were necessary to be fulfilled in order to meet higher needs.

But what if your basic needs are threatened by poverty, or sickness, or physical danger? The problem of suffering in the world is a challenge to belief that God will "graciously give us all things." That is why Paul points to the Cross, the 'emblem of suffering and shame.' (George Bennard) In the Cross God has given us the guarantee of his unfailing love and provision for us. He delivered up his Son to die for us and he suffered in his Son's sufferings. In giving his Son he was giving himself. The self-giving of God in the death of his Son is meant to convince us that he will withhold nothing from us that we really need.

This is dramatized for us in Genesis 22 by the story of Abraham and Isaac. Abraham is called to sacrifice his only son Isaac. In not sparing his own son, Abraham was in effect offering up his own life, his most precious possession, his future, the promise of God to him in the son of his old age. But he did so because he knew that God could even raise Isaac from the dead. God fulfilled his promise to meet Abraham's need in the ram that was supplied for the offering. Abraham called that place *The Lord Will Provide.* This story illustrates that God did not spare himself in his Son. He gave himself. Love is self-giving, love is merciful, love is self-sacrifice. If God would give his own Son, would give himself in his Son, then we may be assured that he will, along with him (his peace, his presence and his power), graciously give us all things.

What are our real needs?

Since God has demonstrated his love in the Cross, no other historical event (whether personal or global) can override or disprove it. No matter what life can throw at us, no matter what circumstances we may find ourselves in, God has promised to give us, with Christ, all that we really need. What are our real needs? Certainly Maslow has identified some of them: acceptance, affirmation, forgiveness, encouragement, significance, courage, faith, hope, love, friendship, security, peace. You may add to those your own list. There is the temptation to meet those needs in material ways. But money cannot buy the answer to any of those needs. Provision for those needs have to be found at a much deeper level. That provision is found in the Christ of the Cross. The story of Ruby Bridges bears this out.

Ruby Bridges was just six years old when in 1960 she stood before a judge who ordered her to go to first grade in the William Franz Elementary School in New Orleans. No black child had ever before stepped foot upon the hallowed white ground.

Every Sunday, her family went to church. Ruby's mother wanted all her children to start feeling close to God's Spirit from the very start. Now, the whole family was praying for strength and courage to get through any 'trouble' as a result of the desegregation ruling. Both her parents were proud that their little daughter had been chosen for such an important event in American history. So, they prayed that she would be a good girl and hold her head up high. They also prayed that Ruby would be a credit to her own people as well as a credit to all the American people.

Federal marshals had to be ordered in by President Dwight D. Eisenhower to escort Ruby into the school building. The New Orleans police as well as the Louisiana police refused their services. Large crowds of angry white people gathered every day outside the school grounds to hurl their epitaphs and threats of physical violence toward Ruby. The marshals carried guns just in case and often threatened arrests to keep the marching crowds back. Ruby would always hurry through them all without saying a word.

Once inside, she took her seat at her desk among a room full of other desks all vacant. None of the white parents would send their children to the school. They all participated in the protest, whether yelling and carrying signs or in the chilly, silent protest of empty desks. No one to learn with. No one to eat with. No one to play with. No one.

However, Ruby had a teacher required by law, Mrs. Henry. She was always dumbfounded by Ruby's politeness and the effectual smile on her face. Wondering how Ruby could keep on going with such a relaxed and hopeful spirit, the teacher speculated when Ruby would wear down or even quit coming altogether. But Ruby said she was doing fine. And so Ruby learned how to read and how to write in an empty classroom in an empty building.

Praying for the people who hated her

Then one morning, Mrs. Henry noticed Ruby walking toward the school as usual but then she stopped, turned toward the angry, howling crowd and seemed to even be trying to speak to them. The crowd seemed ready to pounce on her while the marshals tried in vain to keep Ruby moving. Finally, she stopped talking and walked into the school.

Mrs. Henry immediately asked Ruby what happened; why did she try and talk to such a belligerent crowd. Ruby irritatingly responded that she didn't stop to talk with them. "Ruby, I saw you talking," Mrs. Henry pressed. "I saw your lips moving." "I wasn't talking," said Ruby. "I was praying...I was praying for them." Evidently, Ruby had stopped every morning a few blocks away from the school to pray for the people who hated her. But on this morning she had forgotten until she was already in the middle of the malevolent mob. After school that day, Ruby bolted through the crowd as usual and headed for home with her two companion federal marshals. After a few blocks and with the crowds behind her, she paused as she usually did to say the prayer that she had repeated not once but twice a day -- before and *after* school:

Please God, try to forgive these people.
Because even if they say those bad things,
They don't know what they're doing.
So You could forgive them,
Just like You did those folks a long time ago
When they said terrible things about You.

God met Ruby's needs through Christ's presence with her, his peace within her, and his power to protect her. He is the answer to our real needs.

As St. Patrick prayed:

Christ be with me, Christ within me,
Christ behind me, Christ before me,
Christ beside me, Christ to win me,
Christ to comfort and restore me,
Christ beneath me, Christ above me,
Christ in quiet, Christ in danger,
Christ in hearts of all that love me,
Christ in mouth of friend and stranger.

23

ACCOUNTABILITY

"Who will bring any charge against those whom God has chosen? It is God who justifies. Who is he that condemns? Christ Jesus, who died – more than that, who was raised to life – is at the right hand of God and is also interceding for us." (Romans 8:33,34)

Have you ever been brought up on charges before a court of law? Have you ever thought of standing before the judgment seat of Christ? "For we must all appear before the judgment seat of Christ, that each one may receive what is due him for the things done in the body, whether good or bad." (2 Corinthians 5:10)

It is impossible to appreciate, let alone understand, the teaching of St. Paul if you do not believe that you are accountable to God for your life. Many of our contemporaries feel that they are accountable only to themselves. They are the center of their world, and their goal is to fulfill themselves. They have no obligation to God (if he exists), or to others. They relate to others only to further their own self-realization. In our therapeutic culture when we suffer it is never my fault, for we consider ourselves the victims. We experience power and self-justification when we can blame others for our problems. Gregory Jones opines, "Whoever can claim the status of victim with greater authority wins, because that status projects an image of innocence over against which all others are somehow guilty."[1]

A no-fault society

Crime is explained, not in terms of individual responsibility, but genetic or environmental causes. So sin is not my fault. Nobody can ever be said to be guilty, because nobody has a free choice to do anything. Ultimately I am the victim of my own genetic make-up. "It would seem that we move ever closer to a society free from personal guilt, free from the traditional language of sin…We seek not salvation – as defined in a religious manner – but liberation, as defined psychologically, 'the feeling, the momentary illusion, of personal well-being, health, and psychic security.'"[2]

But personal liberation is hard to come by, because every human being carries within himself, a conviction that he is less than he should or could be - a sense of shame - of failure to live up to what he conceives to be his ideal self. This sickness of the soul condemns him to a sense of deficiency, even if he attempts to ignore God. If you are not accountable to God, you end up being accountable to

---

[1] L.Gregory Jones, *Embodying Forgiveness*, Eerdmans, Grand Rapids, 1995, 46

[2] Alan Mann, *Atonement for a 'Sinless' Society*, Paternoster, UK, 2005, 29

yourself, naked to circumstances, vulnerable to the accusations of the devil, and your last state is worse than your first. How can you escape such shame, such condemnation, unless you consider the diagnosis of St. Paul and his prescription of the Gospel.

"Who will bring any charge against those whom God has chosen? It is God who justifies. Who is he that condemns? Christ Jesus, who died – more than that, who was raised to life – is at the right hand of God and is also interceding for us." (Romans 8:33,34)

A theology of feelings not atonement

Michael Horton relates a scene from NBC's *ER* as illustrative of the present culture. "Lying in his hospital bed while he is dying from cancer, a retired police officer confesses to a chaplain his long-held guilt over allowing an innocent man to be framed and executed. He asks, 'How can I ever hope for forgiveness?' and the chaplain replies, 'I think sometimes it's easier to feel guilty than forgiven.' 'Which means *what*?' 'That maybe your guilt over his death has become your reason for living. Maybe you need a new reason to go on.' 'I don't want to "go on,"' says the dying man. 'Can't you see that I'm dying? The only thing that is holding me back is that I'm afraid – I'm afraid of what comes next.' 'What do you think that is?' the chaplain gently inquires. Growing impatient, the man answers, '*You tell me*. Is atonement possible? What does God *want* from me?' After the chaplain replies, 'I think it's up to each one of us to interpret for ourselves what God wants,' the man stares at her in bewilderment. 'So people can do anything? They can rape, they can murder, they can steal – all in the name of God and it's OK?' Growing intense, the dialogue draws to its climax. That's not what I'm saying,' the chaplain responds. 'Then what *are* you saying? Because all I'm hearing is some New Age, God-is-Love, have-it-your-way crap!... No, I don't have time for this now.' 'You don't understand,' the chaplain counters. 'No, *you* don't understand!... I want a real chaplain who believes in a *real* God and a *real* hell!' Missing the point of this man's struggle, the chaplain collects herself and says in the familiar tone of condescension disguised as understanding, 'I hear that you're frustrated, but you need to ask yourself –' 'No,' the man interrupts, 'I don't need to ask myself anything, I need *answers* and all your questions and all your uncertainty are only making things worse.' With no more to evaluate than his tone, she encourages calm. 'I know you're upset,' she begins, provoking his final outburst of frustration: 'God, I need someone who will look me in the eye and tell me how to find forgiveness, because I am running out of time!'"[3]

Salvation not self-help

Modern culture has redefined sin as sickness, and salvation as self-help. Until we have accepted the fact that we have an obligation to God and to others, we cannot understand the Gospel or our own search for fulfillment. Jesus came, not to abolish the Law of God but to fulfill it. He said, "Anyone who breaks one of the least of these

---

[3] Michael Horton, *Christless Christianity: The Alternative Gospel of the American Church*, Baker, Grand Rapids, 2008, 37

commandments and teaches others to do the same will be called least in the kingdom of heaven." (Matthew 5:19) He went on in the Sermon on the Mount to spell out what it meant to keep the commandments, by applying it to the attitude of the heart, as well as one's actions.

God's standards

"I tell you that anyone who is angry with his brother will be subject to judgment… anyone who says, 'You fool!' will be in danger of the fire of hell….go and be reconciled to your brother." (Matt.5:22-24)

"I tell you anyone who looks at a woman lustfully has already committed adultery with her in his heart….Do not resist an evil person. If some one strikes you on the right cheek, turn to him the other also…Give to the one who asks you, and do not turn away from the one who wants to borrow from you…. Love your enemies, and pray for those who persecute you…. Be perfect as your heavenly Father is perfect…

…When you give to the needy, do not let your left hand know what your right hand is doing, so that your giving may be in secret…Do not store up for yourselves treasures on earth…But store up for yourselves treasures in heaven. You cannot serve God and Money….. Do not worry about your life….But seek first God's kingdom and his righteousness and all these things will be given to you as well. Therefore, do not worry about tomorrow….Do not judge, or you too will be judged, For, in the same way you judge others, you will be judged, and the measure you use, it will be measured to you." (Matthew 5-7)

If we read what God means us to be like in these characteristics of the kingdom of heaven, and compare these words of Jesus with our lives, we see how much we fall short. If we were to be indicted for our failures, our selfishness, our indifference, in the court of God's law, or in the court of our own conscience, we would easily be convicted. There is no one who can say that they are good, innocent, and deserve to be acquitted. So much of the suffering of this world, so much violence and cruelty, is due to the evil in human hearts.

Guilty but acquitted

As St. Paul put it, "Now we know that whatever the law says, it says to those under the law, so that every mouth may be silenced and the whole world held accountable to God. Therefore no one will be declared righteous in his sight by observing the law; rather, through the law we become conscious of sin. But now, a righteousness from God, apart from law has been made known, to which the Law and the Prophets testify. This righteousness comes through faith in Jesus Christ to all who believe." (Romans 3:19-22) As a result, we can be acquitted of our guilt and be restored to wholeness. God is a kinder Judge than our hearts. "Whenever our heart condemns us, God is greater than our heart, and he knows everything." (1 John 3:20)

"Who will bring any charge against those whom God has chosen? It is God who justifies. Who is he that condemns? Christ Jesus, who died – more than that, who was raised to life – is at the right hand of God and is also interceding for us." (Romans 8:33,34)

This is the witness of the Prophets as well as the Apostles. "He who vindicates me is near. Who then will bring charges against me? Let us face each other! Who is my accuser? Let him confront me! It is the Sovereign Lord who helps me. Who is he that will condemn me?" (Isaiah 50:8,9)

Jesus died and rose again, and ascended on high to the place of honor, where he intercedes for us in the court of heaven. This is what Job prophesied. "Even now my witness is in heaven; my advocate is on high. My intercessor is my friend as my eyes pour out tears to God; on behalf of a man he pleads with God as a man pleads for his friend." (Job 16:19-21)

As Hebrews 9:25 assures us, "Therefore Jesus is able to save completely those who come to God through him, because he always lives to intercede for them." Jesus intercedes for us in the court of heaven. "If anyone does sin, we have an advocate with the Father, Jesus Christ the righteous." (1 John 2:1)

24

MORE THAN CONQUERORS

"Who shall separate us from the love of Christ? Shall trouble or hardship or persecution or famine or nakedness or danger or sword? As it is written: 'For your sake we face death all day long; we are considered as sheep to be slaughtered.' [Psalm 44:22] No, in all these things we are more than conquerors through him who loved us." (Romans 8:35-37)

"Invictus" is Latin for unconquerable. It is also the title of a poem by W.E. Henley that inspired Nelson Mandela during his years in prison, and that of the movie about the South African Springboks winning the World Cup. Henley writes about his "unconquerable soul."

> In the fell clutch of circumstance
> I have not winced nor cried aloud.
> Under the bludgeonings of chance
> My head is bloody but unbowed……

It matters not how strait the gate,
How charged with punishments the scroll,
I am the master of my fate:
I am the captain of my soul.

St. Paul also maintained an unconquerable soul in prison. How could he survive and flourish when he faced suffering and execution? What could sustain his spirits, and affirm his value? At moments of loneliness in the cell, what could he look forward to?

St. Paul's sufferings

He was a repeat offender, incarcerated more often than he cared to remember. Not that he was a criminal, but because he challenged the popular culture, proclaimed a higher authority than the government, incensed the local pagan priests, took away the profits of those who fed off the misery of others, and helped to free those who were enslaved and abused.

He was physically punished by being flogged with the cat o' nine tails five times. Each time he received 39 lashes. His back had been torn and bloodied until he could not stand upright and his friends had to rescue him and nurse him back from the brink of death. Three times he had been beaten with hard wooden rods. He had been stoned almost to death. He had been shipwrecked three times and left to drown on the open sea.

He had traveled in dangerous parts, crossing rivers and mountains. He had known threats from bandits, strangers, false friends, and gangs on the streets of the cities. He had suffered from hunger and thirst, lack of adequate clothing, freezing cold and searing heat. He lived a harder life than most. (2 Cor.11:23-27)

He had faced all sorts of trouble: mental distress, worries that upset him, disturbed him, afflicted, grieved, saddened, tormented, annoyed, and discouraged him. He had financial troubles, and troubles with colleagues that depressed him. They threatened to separate him from the love of Christ, from the peace that his faith brought.

Yes, he had faced hardship: severe adversity, hurts, difficulties, misfortunes, accidents, mishaps, unexpected blows, reversals, setbacks, tragedies that afflicted him out of the blue.

He had endured persecution: unjustified criticism, attacks, misrepresentations, abuse, bullying, harassment, provocation without cause, injustice and cruelty. Yet, he could still write,

> "Who shall separate us from the love of Christ? Shall trouble or hardship or persecution or famine or nakedness or danger or sword? As it is written: *'For your sake we face death all day long; we are considered as sheep to be slaughtered.'* [Psalm 44:22] No, in all these things we are more than conquerors through him who loved us." (Romans 8:35-37)

In other parts of the world such trouble, hardship and persecution takes the form of famine, nakedness and the sword – physical hunger, vulnerability to theft of one's clothes and other belongings, and even death, torture, and bodily injury.

Paul was familiar with all these things. He knew what he was talking about. He was no armchair theologian speaking from an ivory tower. What gave him his assurance, his courage, his resilience?

The afflictions of Christ

He said that he endured these things for the sake of Christ. He quoted Ps.44:22. The world considers all these sufferings as evidence of being forgotten by God, of being defeated by evil, of being separated from the love of Christ, but Paul sees them as evidence of signs of fellowship with the One who died on the Cross; the One who loved him and all the world. Just as we are considered sheep to be slaughtered, Christ was the Lamb that was slain before the foundation of the world, the One who took our place – "He was oppressed and afflicted, yet he did not open his mouth; he was led like a lamb to the slaughter, and as a sheep before her shearers is silent, so he did not open his mouth." (Isaiah 53:7) This proves God's love for us in Christ more than anything else can do.

We cannot be separated from the love of Christ by trouble, hardship or persecution because that is where the love of Christ lies. It is through such sufferings that salvation is achieved. Albert Camus recognized with Paul that Christ is the solution to the problems of evil and death. "His solution consisted, first, in experiencing them. The god-man suffers too, with patience. Evil and death can no longer be entirely imputed to him since he suffers and dies. The night on Golgotha is so important in the history of man only because, in its shadows, the divinity, ostensibly abandoning its traditional privileges, lived through to the end, despair included, the agony of death. Thus is explained the *Lama sabachthani* and the frightful doubt of Christ in agony."[1]

When we suffer for the sake of Christ, we enter into his sufferings for our sake, which result in a victory over sin, the world, and the devil. By sharing in his sufferings, and becoming one with him in his death by faith, we triumph over death, we conquer mortality, we attain to the resurrection from the dead. (Philippians 3:10)

A conqueror is someone who has overcome opposition by superior strength. William the Conqueror and his Norman invaders overcame King Harold and his Saxon army at the Battle of Hastings in 1066, and won the right to rule England. Julius Caesar announced the victory of Zela by which he concluded the Pontic campaign with the words: "*Vini, Vidi, Vici* – I came, I saw, I conquered." The Roman Emperor Julian the Apostate (331-363), who opposed Christianity, found he could not defeat the Gospel of Christ. His dying words were "*Vicisti, Galilae* – You have conquered, Galilean."

Jesus the Conqueror

Philip Schaff, theologian and church historian (1819-1893) once wrote, "Jesus of Nazareth, without money and arms, conquered more millions than Alexander, Caesar, Muhummad and Napoleon; without science and learning, he shed more light on things human and divine than all the philosophers and scholars combined; without the eloquence of the school, he spoke words of life such as were never spoken before nor since and produced effects that lie beyond

[1] *Essais,* Paris: Gaillimard, 1965, p.444

the reach of orator or poet; without writing a single line, he has set more pens in motion and furnished themes for more sermons, orations, discussions, works of art, learned volumes, and sweet songs of praise than the whole army of great men of ancient and modern times."

Paul claimed that all who are followers of Christ are "more than conquerors" over all troubles and dangers because they can never be separated from the love of Christ. It is the love of Christ that gives us the power to conquer all things.

G.A. Studdert-Kennedy saw indescribable suffering in World War I. This is how he made sense of it and conquered despair.

> So through the clouds of Calvary –
> There shines his face, and I believe that evil dies,
> And good lives on, loves on, and conquers all –
> All wars must end in peace. These clouds are lies.
> They cannot last. The blue sky is the truth.
> For God is Love. Such is my faith, and such
> My reasons for it, and I find them strong
> Enough. And you? You want to argue?
> Well, I can't. It is a choice.
> I choose the Christ.

25

BEING CONVINCED

"For I am convinced that neither death nor life, neither angels nor demons, neither the present nor the future, nor any powers, neither height nor depth, nor anything else in all creation, will be able to separate us from the love of God that is in Christ Jesus our Lord." (Romans 8:38,39)

What do you need to be convinced of something? What does it take to convince you that this hope is real? The act of examining and weighing up has been concluded by the writer, and a firm conviction has already been reached – the all-embracing, unshakeable certainty that has been attained in faith. St. Paul is persuaded, convinced, sure, that nothing can separate us from God's love in Christ.

This kind of certainty does not come easily. When it seems to come easily it smacks of arrogance, of presumption. People can become too sure of themselves and their opinions. Spiritual certainty can be very off-putting. If someone seems to know all the answers it is difficult to have an honest dialogue with them. They put themselves above contradiction. When Job was suffering he did not need his friends to come and tell him what was wrong with him. They claimed to know all the answers to his problems, all the reasons for his suffering. However, if a person genuinely struggles with the doubts and questions that trouble him, looks at all sides of the problems, honestly pursues the truth, and is open to what God may reveal to him through his experience, through the teaching of the Scriptures, and his human knowledge, and reaches some conclusions on which he can take a stand, that conviction may be respected for it is hard-won and not superficial.

Need to know basis

On the other hand, many people are not willing to do the hard work to win through to a conviction on which they can base their lives. Agnosticism is the comfort zone of many, who prefer *not* to know, rather than to have to declare themselves. There are many things of which we can legitimately be unsure. We do not know the answers to everything. But we need to know some things if we are to make sense of our lives. We need to know if there is something more to this life than meets the eye. "Now faith is being sure of what we hope for, and certain of what we do not see." (Hebrews 11:1)

St. Paul is convinced that life is worthwhile, because of the love of God he has experienced in Jesus Christ, who died for his sins. He is convinced that nothing that this world or the next, success or failure, good or evil, heaven or hell, the present or the future, can do to him, can take away from him the eternal source of love that comes from a relationship with Jesus Christ. So convinced is he of this fact that he wants everyone to know it, everyone to share this assurance, that makes life worthwhile and complete.

Conviction born of suffering

Perhaps you have to suffer before you can reach this conviction. Perhaps you have to reach bedrock before you can build a faith that will last. Perhaps you have to come to the end of yourself before you discover your destiny. That was true for Ernest Gordon, who was captured during World War II and sent to work by the Japanese building the Burma railway. The conditions were brutal. The guards would execute any prisoners who appeared to be lagging. Many more men dropped dead from exhaustion, malnutrition, and disease. It is estimated that 80,000 men died building the railway, 393 fatalities for every mile of track.

Phil Yancey[1], summarized Gordon's story. Ernest Gordon felt himself wasting away from a combination of beriberi, worms, malaria, dysentery and typhoid. Paralyzed and unable to eat, he was put in the Death House, where prisoners on the verge of death were laid out in rows until they stopped breathing. His friends rescued him and cared for him in a bamboo addition to their hut.

"The prison camp was a laboratory of survival of the fittest, every man for himself. Prisoners fought over the few scraps of food. Theft was common. Men lived like animals, and hate was the main motivation to stay alive.

---

[1] Philip Yancey, *A Skeptic's Guide to Faith*, Zondervan, Grand Rapids, 2009, 173-176

Recently, though a change had come. During a tool inspection the guard thought that a shovel was missing. He threatened to kill the detail unless the thief confessed. One enlisted man stepped forward, stood at attention and said, "I did it." The guard beat him to death. That evening, when the tools were inventoried again, the work crew discovered a mistake had been made: no shovel was missing. One of the prisoners remembered the saying of Jesus, "Greater love has no one than this, that he lay down his life for his friends." (John 15:13) Attitudes in the camp began to shift. Prisoners started treating the dying with respect, organizing proper funerals and burials, marking each man's grave with a cross. With no prompting, prisoners began looking out for each other rather than themselves. Theft grew increasingly rare.

Gordon sensed the change in a very personal way as two fellow Scots volunteered to come each day and care for him. After weeks of tender care, Gordon put on a little weight and, to his amazement, regained partial use of his legs.

The new spirit continued to spread through the camp:

'Death was still with us – no doubt about that. But we were slowly being freed from its destructive grip. We were seeing for ourselves the sharp contrast between the forces that made for life and those that made for death. Selfishness, hatred, envy, jealousy greed, self-indulgence, laziness and pride were all anti-life. Love, heroism, self-sacrifice, sympathy, mercy, integrity and creative faith, on the other hand, were the essence of life, turning mere existence into living in its truest sense. These were the gifts of God to men…

True, there was hatred. But there was also love. There was death. But there was also life. God had not left us.

He was with us, calling us to live the divine life in fellowship.' (Ernest Gordon, *To End All Wars*, 105ff.)

Faith thrives when there is no hope but God

As Gordon continued to recover, some of the men, knowing he had studied philosophy, asked him to lead a discussion group on ethics. The conversations kept circling around the issue of how to prepare for death, the most urgent question of the camp. Seeking answers, Gordon returned to fragments of faith recalled from his childhood. He had thought little about God for years, but as he would later put it, 'Faith thrives when there is no hope but God.' By default, Gordon became the unofficial camp chaplain. The prisoners built a tiny church, and each evening they gathered to say prayers for those with the greatest needs.

Gordon's books (*Miracle on the River Kwai*, and *To End All Wars*) tell of the transformation of individual men in the camp, a transformation so complete that when liberation finally came the prisoners treated their sadistic guards with kindness and not revenge. Gordon's life was changed. As a result of his experiences he gave his life to sharing the love of God in Christ with others. He became a Presbyterian minister and ended up as the Dean of the Chapel at Princeton University."

Ernest Gordon was convinced that nothing could separate him from the love of God that is in Jesus Christ who became his Lord and Savior. St. Paul was convinced. Of what are you convinced? Are you convinced of the transforming love of Christ? Have you examined and weighed up the evidence for it. Where are you on your search? Can you reach a conclusion and a firm conviction? May the all-embracing, unshakeable certainty of St. Paul be yours as well.

EPILOGUE

THE GOD OF HOPE

"May the God of hope fill you with all joy and peace as you trust in him, so that you may overflow with hope by the power of the Holy Spirit." (Romans 15:13)

I close this book with a prayer, or benediction, that you may overflow with hope by the power of the Holy Spirit. What a wonderful way to conclude this journey.

How we view and experience the character of God determines our own spiritual health. All too often we craft God in our own image – of what we want God to be for us. Or we reject the image of God that has been modeled to us by the culture and the authority figures in our lives. But God is above and beyond us – God is an objective reality, not just a subjective construct. God is also nearer to us than our own breath. "God is not far from each one of us. For in him we live and move and have our being." (Acts 17:27,28) He is both transcendent (existing apart from us, not subject to the limitations of the material universe), and also immanent (indwelling us).

Eric Milner White wrote,

The men of science measure space, measure
aeons, measure force:
they cannot measure righteousness,
nor wisdom, nor love.
No equation, no research, no guess even, can
reach a majesty so distant and so close.
You who are high above all, always,
does yet ask room within;
By might of creation, you are our Father
but yet more mightily by love.[1]

J.B. Phillips in *"Your God is Too Small"* lists 13 destructive views of God. Our early conception of God is founded upon our experience of our parents. If there have been traumatic events, abuse, violence, or emotional absence, then we may view God as either indifferent to us or to be feared. If we were raised in stained-glass churches where worship was conducted in archaic language and old-fashioned music, then our view of God may be similarly colored. If the sermons were couched in theological jargon and aimed at an academic audience then God may be seen to live in an ivory tower and not be in touch with our actual lives. At the opposite end of the spectrum, some over-familiar presentations may cheapen our understanding of God.

The God of Perfection may be so unreachable as to be uncomfortable to associate with and may lead us to despair. So many representations of religion in the media are distorted and unreal. They set up God as straw men to be knocked down with contempt. God may be presented as an impersonal Fate that has no feelings for us. For others, God

---

[1] *My God, My Glory*, SPCK, London, 1994, p.133

is the Great Disappointment, as someone not to be trusted: "I prayed, but God let me down!" God has failed us. We can nurture a perennial grievance against him. It gives us a good reason to cut God down to our size. We feel that he owes us, and that we have no obligation to him. To this way of thinking, God has much to answer for, if he exists! Blaming God for all our ills is an easy way to avoid personal responsibility.

Caricatures of God versus Character of God

Of course, the lives of many professing Christians present a view of God that is far from attractive. They may be insipid, pale reflections of a robust faith. For others, God is a Spoilsport, out to deny us any happiness. Or they say that God is a Dictator, who takes pleasure in telling us what to do, and seeking to micro-manage our lives so that we have no time for our own enjoyment. All the above are caricatures of what God is really like.

The Bible gives us a picture of the character of God that is comprehensive. Jesus came to reveal that God is our Father, a personal God who wants to live with us, and through us. St. Paul found that he could not find enough words to describe God. Using Isaiah 40:13 and Job 41:11 he bursts into a doxology of praise:

> Oh, the depth of the riches of the wisdom and knowledge of God!
> How unsearchable his judgments, and his paths beyond tracing out!

> Who has known the mind of the Lord? Or who has been his counselor?
> Who has ever given to God, that God should repay him?
> For from him and through him and to him are all things.
> To him be the glory forever! Amen. (Romans 11:33-35)

Hope or Despair

God is the only One who can give hope, sustain hope, crown hope, for he is eternal and he is love. Hope looks forward to the future. Paul looks forward to the future with a glory that will be revealed in a new universe which those who have faith in Christ will one day assuredly inherit. God is not the bringer of despair, but the conveyor of hope. Absence of a relationship with the God and Father of our Lord Jesus Christ, can only bring an agnosticism that results in despair. You either believe in a God of hope, or a black hole of nothingness, which brings despair. Those who despair easily have not met with Jesus. Those who have no hope are unable to trust anyone.

Faith and hope go together. If you can trust in Christ, the revealer of the God of hope, you can look forward to a glorious future. You can face the future with a spirit of optimism. "Pessimism is altogether alien from the true Christian spirit. A Christian will always be an optimist, not in a superficial, sentimental sense, but because of the great stronghold of hope which is his in Christ." (W.H. Griffith Thomas)

As you trust in, believe in, God, as revealed in Jesus Christ, the God of hope will fill you with all joy and peace. Joy is energetic, peace is restful. The joy of the Lord is our strength. Peace is the great word of harmony, wholeness, and reconciliation. God wants to fill us with joy and peace. God is not content with handing out small portions of his grace. He wants us to know the abundance that he has in store for us.

I want to experience the fullness of joy and peace. When I don't, I experience anxiety, dread, fear, the premonition of disaster. The only antidote for me is to trust in the God of hope. Joy and peace is the result of trust in Christ. When I am not placing my faith and trust in Jesus I lose my joy and peace. I am lost in anxiety, lost in despair, lost in depression.

Joy in being found

Jesus told the parables of the lost sheep, the lost coin, and the lost son, to illustrate the joy of finding something precious that was lost. The shepherd is filled with joy over finding his lost sheep. The woman is filled with joy when she found her lost coin. The father is filled with joy when his prodigal son returns home. "In the same way, I tell you, there is rejoicing in heaven, in the presence of the angels of God, over one sinner who repents." (Luke 15:7,10,32) That joy should be ours when we find that we can trust in the God and Father of our Lord Jesus Christ, because he is the God of hope – he fulfills his promises in the future. We should not despair. Instead we have every reason to hope.

Paul reminds us that the peace of God which transcends all understanding, will guard our hearts and minds in Christ Jesus if we fight anxiety with prayer and petition, with thanksgiving. (Philippians 4:6,7) Peace is ours when we find that we can bring our anxieties to God in prayer with thanksgiving, because we trust in Christ Jesus who reveals to us that God is a God of hope.

The fullness of joy and peace is not achieved by an act of the will. It is the gift of the Holy Spirit. For the God of hope is brought to us by the power of the Holy Spirit. Paul prays that we may "overflow with hope by the power of the Holy Spirit."

To be indwelt by the God of hope, to overflow with hope, requires an opening of our heart and mind to the power of the Holy Spirit. It is a supernatural energy that enables us to experience hope. It is not a natural gritting of our teeth in the face of adversity. Hope does not come to us as a result of endurance. Hope is the product of the overflowing of the Holy Spirit. Therefore, we should seek the filling of the Spirit every day. "We who have fled to take hold of the hope offered to us may be greatly encouraged. We have this hope as an anchor for the soul, firm and secure." (Hebrews 6:18,19)

The God of hope is the God and Father of our Lord Jesus Christ, revealed to us by Jesus, and given to us by the Holy Spirit. This is the true God revealed to us in the Scriptures. He wants to bring us joy and peace as we trust in him. "For everything that was written in the past was written to teach us, so that through endurance and the encouragement of the Scriptures we might have hope." (Romans 15:4)

TED SCHRODER,

is pastor of Amelia Plantation Chapel, Amelia Island, Florida and has ministered in London, Massachusetts, Texas and Florida to churches and colleges. He is married to Antoinette Bowie Schroder, and has two daughters and three grandchildren. He can be reached by email at *tschroder@ameliachapel*. You can sign up for his blog at *www.ameliachapel.com/blog*.

CPSIA information can be obtained at www.ICGtesting.com
Printed in the USA
LVOW060821250412

279059LV00001B/1/P

9 780974 808666